Carols Old and New

100 Settings for S.A. and Men

Compiled by
Malcolm Archer & Alan Ridout

Kevin Mayhew

We hope you enjoy the music in *Carols Old and New.*
Further copies are available from your local music or christian bookshop.

In case of difficulty, please contact the publisher direct:

The Sales Department
KEVIN MAYHEW LTD
Rattlesden
Bury St Edmunds
Suffolk IP30 0SZ

Phone   0449 737978
Fax   0449 737834

Please ask for our complete catalogue of outstanding
Church Music.

First published in Great Britain by
KEVIN MAYHEW LTD
Rattlesden
Bury St Edmunds
Suffolk IP30 0SZ

ISBN 0 86209 247 7

Cover design: Graham Johnstone
Music setting: Musicprint, London
Printed and bound by Bath Press, Bath

Contents

Acknowledgements

The publishers wish to express their gratitude to the following for
permission to use copyright material in this book:

The Rt. Rev'd. Timothy Dudley-Smith, 9 Ashlands, Ford, Salisbury, Wiltshire SP4 6DY for:
See, to us a child is born (words) © Timothy Dudley-Smith

Herald Music Service, 28 Church Circle, Farnborough, Hampshire for:
Good King Wenceslas (arrangement)

Jubilate Hymns Ltd, 61 Chessel Avenue, Southampton SO2 4DY for:
Come, all you good people from an old Dorset carol (words) © Michael Saward/Jubilate Hymns
Christmas for God's holy people (words) © Michael Saward/Jubilate Hymns
Behold, the great Creator (words)

Magdalene College, Cambridge for: *Whence is that goodly fragrance flowing* (translation)

Oxford University Press, Walton Street, Oxford OX2 6DP for:
When Jesus Christ was yet a child (translation) from *Oxford Book of Carols.*

Oxford University Press, 7-8 Hatherley Street, London SW1P 2QT for: *O little town of Bethlehem*
(melody collection and adaptation by R Vaughan Williams from the *English Hymnal*)

Royal School of Church Music, Addington Palace, Croydon, Surrey CR9 5AD for:
O little town of Bethlehem (descant by Thomas Armstrong)

Stainer & Bell Ltd, PO Box 110, 82 High Road, East Finchley, London N2 9PW for:
Christmas for God's Holy People (music)

Every effort has been made to trace the owners of copyright material, and we hope that no
copyright has been infringed. Pardon is sought and apology made if the contrary be the case,
and a correction will be made in any reprint of this book.
All other works in *Carols Old and New* are © Copyright Kevin Mayhew Ltd.

Foreword

Such was the critical and popular acclaim which greeted the
original SATB edition of *Carols Old and New* it quickly became
clear that further editions for other combinations of voices would
find a similarly enthusiastic welcome. Hence the present collection
for choirs which are rather short of men – the SA Men edition.

When we began work on the original *Carols Old and New* we knew
clearly the kind of music we wanted to include: traditional carols in
new clothes which fitted well and were a joy to wear, and carols
which, while being recognisably of the twentieth century, took into
account the tradition and ethos of Christmas. We were concerned
to preserve the unique appeal of the carol, of which Frank Howes
has written: 'Musically the carol . . . has united scholars,
ecclesiastics, musicians and the great public, including the
unmusical, into a fellowship unparalleled in the realm of music'.
(The English Musical Renaissance)

A dedicated team of composers and arrangers provided us with
settings that were authentic, musicianly and a pleasure to perform.
It seemed sensible in view of the success of their original efforts to
invite the same people to write for the present edition. We have
also taken the opportunity to include some new composers and
once again we thank them all and pay tribute to the consummate
skills of our colleagues who have contributed to the book.

Carols Old and New has been a joy to bring to birth. We hope
countless numbers of the 'fellowship unparalleled' will share
our delight.

MALCOLM ARCHER
ALAN RIDOUT

1

For Sara and Edward

WHEN CHRIST WAS BORN OF MARY FREE

Text: From a 15th *c.* Manuscript
Music: Christopher Tambling (*b.*1964)

1. When Christ was born of Ma-ry free, in Beth-lem in that fair ci-ty, an-gels sung e'er with mirth and glee, 'In ex-cel-sis glo-ri-a.'

2. Herd-men be-held these an-gels bright, to them ap-pear-ed with great light, and said, 'God's son is born this night: In ex-cel-sis glo-ri-a.'

3. This king is come to save his kind, in the scrip-ture as we find, there-fore this song have we in mind: 'In ex-cel-sis glo-ri - a.'

4. Then, dear Lord, for thy great grace, grant us the bliss to see thy face where we may sing to thy so - lace: 'In ex - cel - sis glo - ri - a.'

2

COVENTRY CAROL

Text: Robert Croo (*c.*1534)
Music: Pageant of the Shearmen and Tailors (15 *c.*)
arranged by Dom Gregory Murray (1905-1992)

If all the F sharps in this melody are sung as F naturals, its original modal form can be restored.

9

3

For Catharine

HARK, HOW ALL THE WELKIN RINGS!

Text: Charles Wesley (1707-1788)
Music: Richard Lloyd (*b.*1933)

u - ni - ver - sal na-ture say 'Christ the Lord is born to-day.'

Altos *mf*

2. Christ, by high - est heav'n a - dored,

Man.

Sopranos

Christ, the e - ver - last - ing Lord, late in time be - hold him come, off-spring of a

Ped.

Altos
mp
cresc.

vir-gin's womb. Veiled in flesh, the god-head see! Hail the'in-car-nate de - i -ty!

mp
cresc.

Man.

Pleased as man with men to 'ap-pear, Je - sus, our Em - man-uel here!

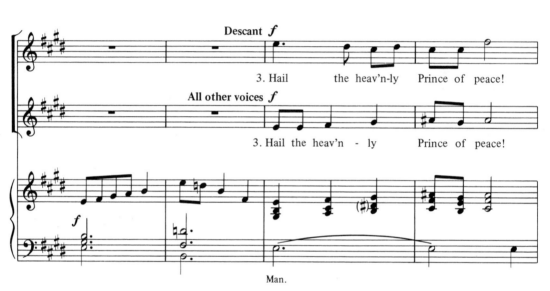

Descant *f*
3. Hail the heav'n-ly Prince of peace!

All other voices *f*
3. Hail the heav'n - ly Prince of peace!

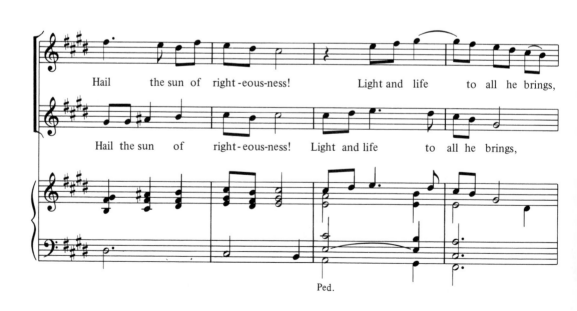

Hail the sun of right-eous-ness! Light and life to all he brings,

Hail the sun of right-eous-ness! Light and life to all he brings,

ris'n with heal - ing in his wings. Mild he lays his glo - ry by,

ris'n with heal - ing in his wings. Mild he lays his glo - ry by,

born that man no more may die, born to raise

born that man no more may die, born to raise the

the sons of earth, born to give them se - cond birth!

sons of earth, born to give them se - cond birth!

† take convenient note

re - con - ciled.' Joy - ful, ye na - tions,

re - con - ciled.' Joy - ful, all ye na - tions, rise,

join the tri - umph; 'Christ is

join the tri - umph of the skies; u - ni - ver - sal

born, Christ the Lord is born to - day.'

na - ture say 'Christ the Lord is born to - day.'

rall.

4

GOOD KING WENCESLAS

Text: from *Piae Cantiones* (1582) translated by John Mason Neale (1818-1866)
Music: Traditional English Melody arranged by Colin Mawby (*b.*1936)

1. Good King Wen - ces - las looked out on the Feast of Ste - phen,
2. 'Hi - ther, page, and stand by me, if thou know'st it, tell - ing;
3. 'Bring me flesh and bring me wine, bring me pine logs hi - ther;
4. 'Sire, the night is dark - er now, and the wind blows strong - er;
5. In his mas - ter's steps he trod where the snow lay dint - ed;

when the snow lay round a - bout, deep, and crisp, and e - ven:
yon - der pea - sant, who is he, where and what his dwell - ing?'
thou and I will see him dine when we bear them thi - ther.'
fails my heart, I know not how; I can go no long - er.'
heat was in the ve - ry sod which the saint had print - ed.

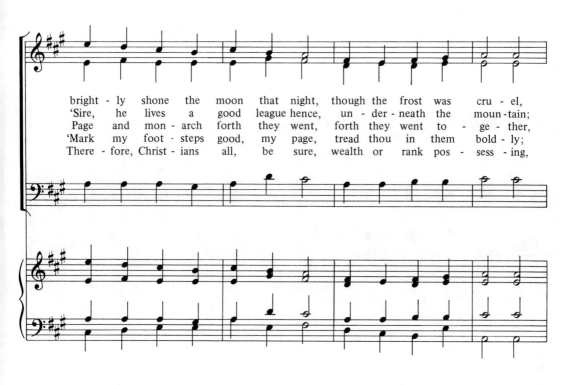

bright - ly shone the moon that night, though the frost was cru - el,
'Sire, he lives a good league hence, un - der - neath the moun - tain;
Page and mon - arch forth they went, forth they went to - ge - ther,
'Mark my foot - steps good, my page, tread thou in them bold - ly;
There - fore, Christ - ians all, be sure, wealth or rank pos - sess - ing,

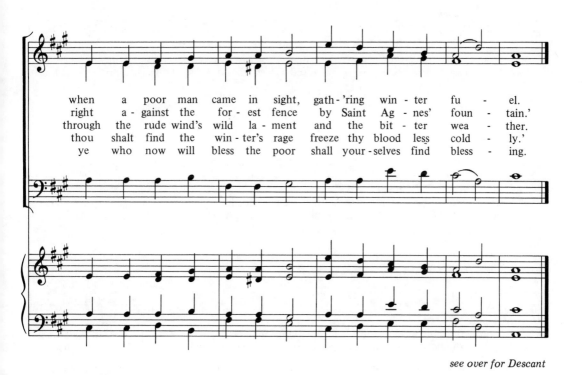

when a poor man came in sight, gath - 'ring win - ter fu - el.
right a - gainst the for - est fence by Saint Ag - nes' foun - tain.'
through the rude wind's wild la - ment and the bit - ter wea - ther.
thou shalt find the win - ter's rage freeze thy blood less cold - ly.'
ye who now will bless the poor shall your - selves find bless - ing.

see over for Descant

Alternative ending for verse 5

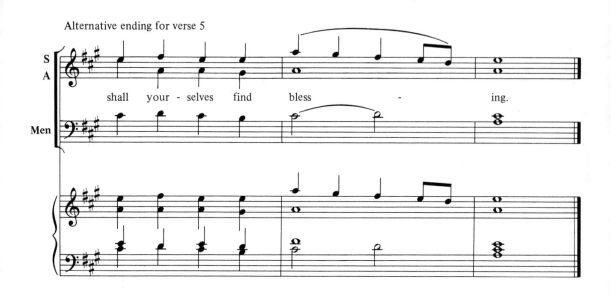

shall your - selves find bless - ing.

Descant*

3. 'Bring me flesh, and bring me wine, bring me pine logs hi - ther:
5. In his mas - ter's steps he trod where the snow lay dint - ed;

thou and I will see him dine, when we bear them thi - ther.'
heat was in the ve - ry sod which the saint had print - ed.

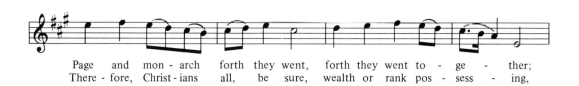

Page and mon - arch forth they went, forth they went to - ge - ther;
There - fore, Christ - ians all, be sure, wealth or rank pos - sess - ing,

through the rude wind's wild la - ment and the bit - ter wea - ther.
ye who now will bless the poor shall your - selves find bless - ing.

* If this carol is sung in dialogue form, the descant should be sung to verse 5 and the alternative ending omitted.

5

GALLERY CAROL

Text: Based on a Dorset Carol by Michael Saward (*b.*1932)
Music: Traditional English Melody arranged by Stanley Vann (*b.*1910)

mem - ber the birth-day of Je - sus our king, who brings us sal - va - tion; his

glo - ry we sing.

Sopranos *p*

2. His

mf

p

mo - ther, a vir - gin so gen - tle and pure, was told of God's pro - mise un -

chang - ing and sure, fore - tell - ing the birth - day of Je - sus our king, who

brings us sal - va - tion: his glo - ry we sing.

3. To Beth - le - hem hur - ried the shep - herds a - mazed, with

Men *mf*

Man.

sto - ries of an - gels and hea - vens that blazed, pro - claim - ing the birth - day of

Ped.

Je - sus our king, who brings us sal - va - tion: his glo - ry we sing.

f poco meno mosso
4. So come, hon - our the

4. So come, let us hon - our the

f

poco rall.

poco meno mosso

f

babe in the hay, and give him our hom-age and

babe in the hay, and give him our hom-age and

wor-ship to-day, the birth - day of Je-sus our king,

wor-ship to-day, re-call-ing the birth-day of Je-sus our king who

rall. e cresc.

S

cresc. our Je-sus: his glo - ry we sing.

A

brings us sal - va - tion: his glo ry we sing.

cresc.

Ten

rall.

cresc.

23

6

CHILD IN THE MANGER

Text: Mary Macdonald (1817-1890) translated by Lachlan Macbean (1853-1931)
Music: Traditional Gaelic Melody arranged by Malcolm Archer (*b.* 1952)

1. Child in the man - ger, in - fant of Ma - ry; out - cast and
2. Once that most ho - ly child of sal - va - tion gen - tle and

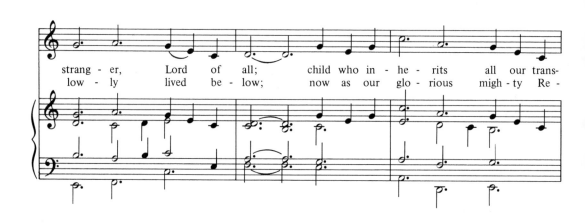

strang - er, Lord of all; child who in - he - rits all our trans-
low - ly lived be - low; now as our glo - rious migh - ty Re -

gres - sions, all our de - me - rits on him fall.
deem - er, see him vic - tor - ious o'er each foe.

Descant

3. Pro - phets fore - told him, in - fant of won - der; an - gels be -

All other voices

3. Pro - phets fore - told him, in - fant of won - der; an - gels be -

hold him on his throne; wor - thy our Sa - viour of all their

hold him on his throne; wor - thy our Sa - viour of all their

prai - ses; hap - py for e - ver are his own.

prai - ses; hap - py for e - ver are his own.

7

For Emma

ANGELS FROM THE REALMS OF GLORY

Text: James Montgomery (1771-1854)
Music: Traditional French Melody arranged by Richard Lloyd (*b.* 1933)

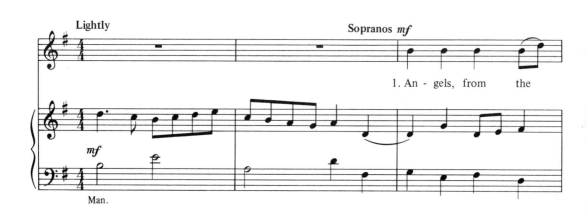

Refrain

Come and wor - ship Christ the new - born King, come and wor - ship, wor - ship Christ the new - born King.

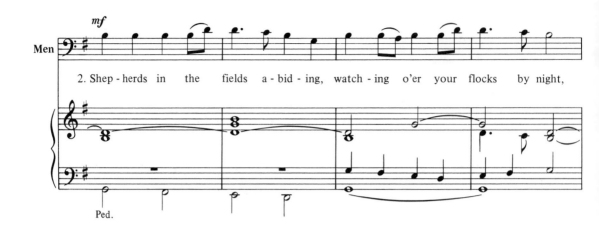

2. Shep - herds in the fields a - bid - ing, watch - ing o'er your flocks by night,

Ped.

God with man is now re - sid - ing; yon - der shines the in - fant Light:

Refrain

Come and wor - ship

Christ the new-born King, come

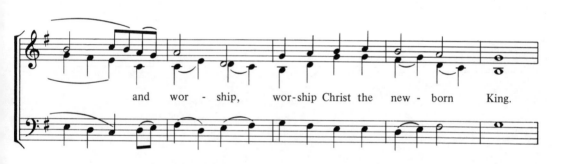

and wor - ship, wor-ship Christ the new - born King.

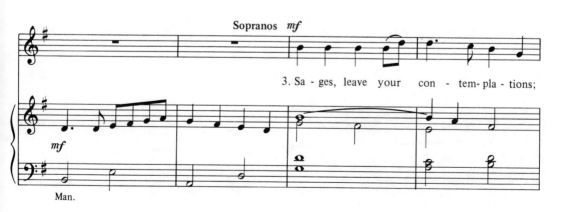

3. Sa - ges, leave your con - tem - pla - tions;

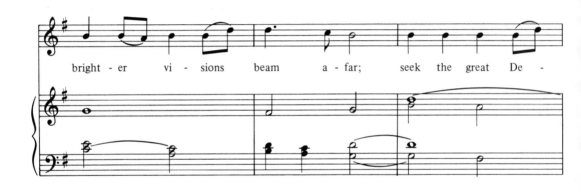

bright - er vi - sions beam a - far; seek the great De -

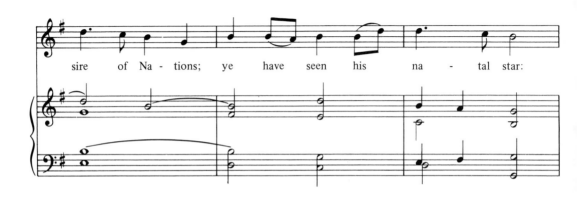

sire of Na - tions; ye have seen his na - tal star:

Refrain

A

Come and wor - ship

Men

Ped.

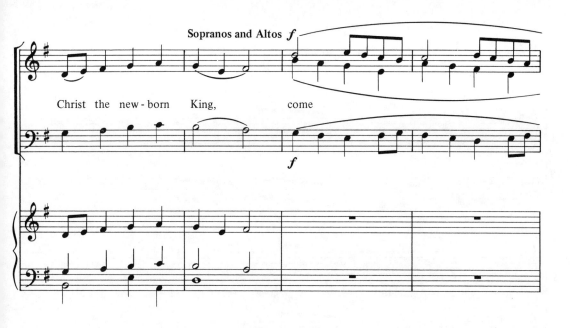

Sopranos and Altos *f*

Christ the new-born King, come

f

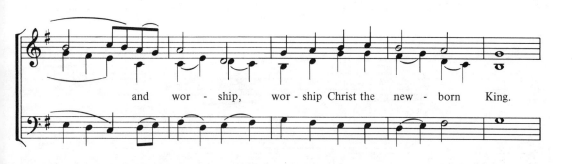

and wor - ship, wor - ship Christ the new - born King.

All *mp*

4. Though an in - fant now we view him,

mp

Man.

31

he shall fill his Fa - ther's throne, ga - ther all the

na - tions to him; ev - 'ry knee shall then bow down:

Refrain
Sopranos
mf

Come   and

wor - ship Christ the new - born King,

32

come,   come,   come   and

come   and

wor - ship,   wor - ship Christ,   the   new - born

wor - ship,

wor - ship Christ   the   new - born   King.

allarg. **ff**

King,   wor - ship Christ the   new - born   King.

allarg. **ff**

8

THE HOLLY AND THE IVY

Text: English Traditional Carol collected by Cecil Sharp (1859-1924)
Music: English Traditional Melody arranged by Richard Lloyd (*b.* 1933)

To Refrain

Ma - ry bore sweet Je - sus Christ to be our sweet Sa - viour.

Solo Soprano
mp

3. The hol - ly bears a ber - ry as red as a - ny blood, and

Solo
mp

To Refrain

Ma - ry bore sweet
Ma - ry bore sweet Je - sus Christ to do poor sin - ners good.

Solo *mp*

4. The hol - ly bears a prick - le as sharp as a - ny thorn, and

Solo
mp

To Refrain

Ma - ry bore sweet Je - sus Christ on Christ-mas Day in the morn.

see over for verse 5

35

9
FOLLOWING ALONG

Text: Michael Forster (*b.*1946)
Music: Traditional French Melody arranged by John Jordan (*b.*1941)

road where the ho - ly cou - ple trod, share the
road where the shep - herds went be - fore, called to
road where a star leads through the night. Bring our -
road where a pil - grim host has passed; saints who

Share the jour - ney fol - low - ing a - long fol - low - ing

road. Share the jour - ney: fol - low - ing a - long. Set our

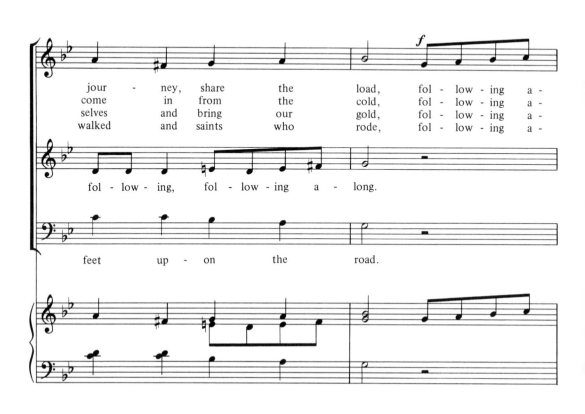

jour - ney, share the load, fol - low - ing a -
come in from the cold, fol - low - ing a -
selves and bring our gold, fol - low - ing a -
walked and saints who rode, fol - low - ing a -

fol - low - ing, fol - low - ing a - long.

feet up - on the road.

long,   fol-low-ing a - long, share the jour - ney, share the
long,   fol-low-ing a - long, called to come in from the
long,   fol-low-ing a - long, bring our - selves and bring our
long,   fol-low-ing a - long, saints who walked and saints who

fol - low - ing a - long, a - long, fol - low-ing, fol - low-ing, fol-low-ing a-

fol - low-ing a - long, set our feet up - on the

load on a pil - grim - age with God.
cold through an e - ver o - pen door.
gold to a man - ger filled with light.
rode, to a - dore the First and Last.

long, fol - low-ing fol - low-ing a - long.

road, fol - low-ing, fol - low-ing a - long.

39

10

WHAT CHILD IS THIS

Text: William Chatterton Dix (1837-1898)
Music: Traditional English Melody arranged by Richard Lloyd (*b.*1933)

1. What child is this, who, laid to rest, on Ma – ry's lap is
2. Why lies he in such mean es - tate, where ox and ass are

sleep – ing? Whom an - gels greet with an - thems sweet, while
feed – ing? Good Christ - ians, fear! for sin - ners here the

shep – herds watch are keep – ing? This, this is
si - lent Word is plead – ing. Nails, spear shall

Christ the king, whom shep-herds guard and an-gels sing:
pierce him through, the cross be borne for me, for you:

D.C.

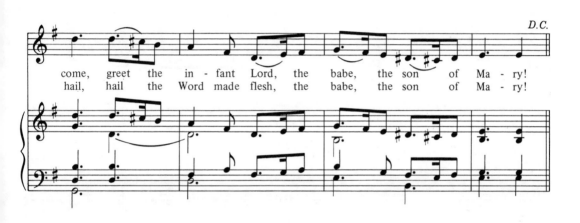

come, greet the in-fant Lord, the babe, the son of Ma-ry!
hail, hail the Word made flesh, the babe, the son of Ma-ry!

Descant

3. So bring him in-cense, gold and myrrh, all tongues and peo-ples own him. The

All other voices

3. So bring him in-cense, gold and myrrh, all tongues and peo-ples own him. The

King of kings, let ev-'ry heart en-throne him:

King of kings sal-va-tion brings, let ev-'ry heart en-throne him:

raise, raise your song on high, while Ma-ry sings a lul-la-by;

raise, raise your song on high, while Ma-ry sings a lul-la-by;

joy, joy for Christ is born, the babe, the son of Ma - ry.

joy, joy for Christ is born, the babe, the son of Ma - ry.

11
WE THREE KINGS

Text and Music: John Henry Hopkins (1820-1891)
arranged by Colin Mawby (b.1936)

1. We three kings of O - ri - ent are; bear - ing

gifts we tra - vel a - far: field and foun - tain,

moor and moun - tain, fol - low - ing yon - der star.

Refrain

O star of won - der, star of night,

Ped.

star with roy - al beau - ty bright: west - ward lead - ing,

still pro - ceed - ing, guide us to thy per - fect light.

Verse 2

Man.

Melchior (**Solo or all men**)

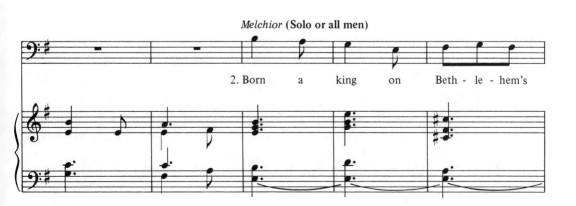

2. Born a king on Beth - le - hem's

plain, gold I bring, to crown him a - gain: King for

e - ver, ceas - ing ne - ver, o - ver us all to reign.

D.S. To Refrain

Verse 3

Caspar (**Solo or all men**)

3. Frank - in - cense to of - fer have

Man.

I, in - cense owns a de - i - ty nigh: prayer and

praising, all men rais - ing, wor - ship him, God most high!

Verse 4

Balthazar **(Solo or all men)**

4. Myrrh is mine; its bit- ter per -

Man.

Ped.

fume breathes a life of ga - ther-ing gloom: sor - row-ing,

D.S. *To Refrain*

sigh - ing, bleed - ing, dy - ing, sealed in the stone - cold tomb.

Verse 5

Descant

Ah

All other voices

5. Glo - rious now be - hold him a -

Man.

Ped.

Ah

Al - le -

rise, King and God and sac - ri - fice! Heav'n sings:

lu - ia, Al - le - lu - ia, Al - le - lu - ia!

'Al - le - lu - ia!' 'Al - le - lu - ia!' the earth re - plies.

O _____ star of won - der, star of night,

O _____ star of won - der, star of night,

star with roy - al beau - ty bright: west - ward lead - ing,

star with roy - al beau - ty bright: west - ward lead - ing,

still pro - ceed - ing, guide us to thy per - fect light.

still pro - ceed - ing, guide us to thy per - fect light.

12
BEHOLD, THE GREAT CREATOR

Text: Thomas Pestel (1584-1659), alt. Jubilate Hymns
Music: Neil Dougall (1776-1862) arranged by Philip Moore (*b.*1943)

1. Be-hold, the great Cre-a-tor makes him-self a house of

clay; a robe of hu-man form he takes for

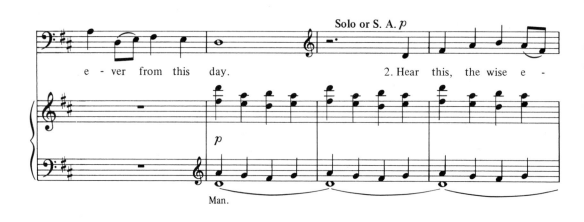

e-ver from this day. 2. Hear this, the wise e-

Man.

ter-nal Word as Ma-ry's in-fant cries; a ser-vant is our

might - y Lord, and God in cra - dle lies.

All *mf*

3. Glad

shep - herds run to view this sight, a choir of an - gels

sings; wise men from far with pure de - light a -

dore the King of kings.

4. These won-ders all the

world a - maze and shake the star - ry frame; the

host of hea - ven stand to gaze, and bless the Sa - viour's

13

For the organist and choir of St. John's Church, Buxton

THIS IS THE TRUTH SENT FROM ABOVE

Text: Traditional, collected by E.M. Leather
Music: English Traditional Melody arranged by Richard Lloyd (*b.*1933)

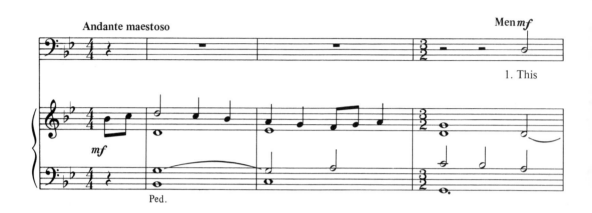

heark-en all, both rich and poor.   2. The

Man.

first thing which I do re-late is that God did

man cre-ate; the next thing which to you I'll tell; wo -

man was made with man to dwell.   3. Thus we were heirs to

Ped.

55

end -less woes till God the Lord did in -ter -pose; and so a pro - mise

4. And
Sopranos *pp*

soon did run that he would re - deem us by his Son.

at that sea - son of the year our blest Re - deem - er
(hum)

did ap - pear; he here did live and here did preach, and
(hum)

ma - ny thou - sands he did teach.
(hum)

largando
f Descant
5. Thus he in love to us be - haved,
(hum)
f All other voices
5. Thus he in love to us be - haved, to
largando
mf
Ped.
to show how we must be saved; and if you want to
show us how we must be saved; and if you want to
ff molto allarg.
know the way, be pleas'd to hear what he did say.
ff
know the way, be pleas'd to hear what he did say.
molto allarg.
ff

14

THE ANGEL GABRIEL

Text: Sabine Baring-Gould (1834-1924)
Music: Basque Folk Melody arranged by Richard Lloyd (*b.* 1933)

1. The an-gel Ga-bri-el from hea-ven came, his wings as drift-ed snow, his eyes as flame; 'All hail,' said he, 'thou low-ly maid-en Ma - ry, most

2. 'For known a bless-ed mo-ther thou shalt be; all ge-ne-ra-tions laud and hon - our thee. Thy Son shall be Em-man-u - el, by seers fore-told, most

3. Then gen-tle Ma-ry meek-ly bowed her head, 'To me be as it pleas-eth God,' she said, 'My soul shall laud and mag-ni-fy his ho - ly name.' 'Most

high - ly fa - voured la - dy.' Glo - ri - a!

high - ly fa - voured la - dy.' Glo - ri - a!

Descant

4. Of her the Christ was born, in

Melody

4. Of her Em-man - u - el the Christ was born, in

Ped.

Beth - le - hem, on Christ - mas morn, and

Beth - le - hem, all on a Christ - mas morn, and

Christ - ian folk will e - ver say,

Christ - ian folk through-out the world will e - ver say, 'most

S

'most high - ly fa - voured: Glo - ri - a!'

A

high - ly fa-voured la - dy, Glo - ri - a!'

Men

high - ly fa-voured la - dy, Glo - ri - a!'

rall.

15

To Esther de Waal

CELTIC CAROL

Text: adapted from the *Carmina Gadelica*
Music: Alan Ridout (b.1934)

This is the eve of Na - ti - vi - ty, Ha ri vi ho hu,

this night is born Ma-ry's Son, Ha ri vi ho hu. This night is born Je - sus,

Hu ri vi ho hu. This night is born the root of our joy,

Ha ri vi ho hu. Gleamed the sun and the shore to - ge - ther,

Ha ri vi ho hu, this night was born Christ the King,

16

For Colin Walsh and Lincoln Cathedral Choir

IN DULCI JUBILO

Text: Translated from the German by Robert Lucas Pearsall (1795-1856)
Music: Melody from Klug's *Geistliche Lieder,* 1535 (but earlier)
arranged by Malcolm Archer (*b.*1952)

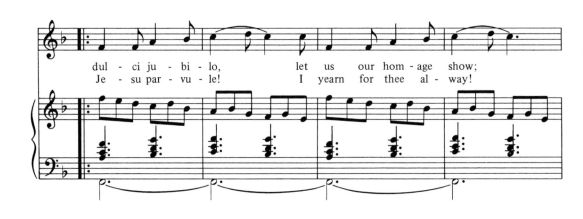

dul - ci ju - bi - lo, let us our hom - age show;
Je - su par - vu - le! I yearn for thee al - way!

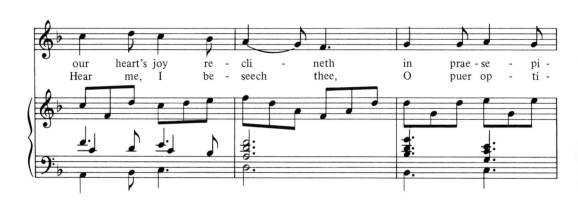

our heart's joy re - cli - neth in prae - se - pi -
Hear me, I be - seech thee, O puer op - ti -

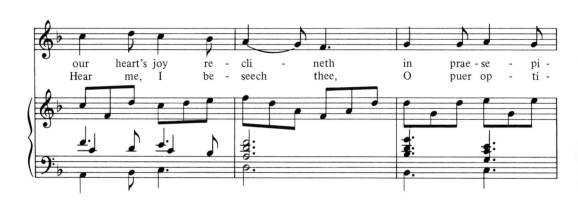

o.   and like a bright star shi - neth ma - tris in gre - mi -
me! My pray - er let it reach thee, O Prin - ceps glo - ri -

o.   Al - pha es et O,   Al - pha es et
ae! Tra - he me post te!   Tra - he me post

O.   1.   *f* Men
te!   2. O

2.

Solo or All *mp*

3. O Pa - tris ca - ri - tas, O Na - ti le - ni -

tas! Deep - ly were we stain - ed per nos - tra cri - mi -

na; but thou hast for us gai - ned cæ -

lo - rum gau - di - a. O that we were

67

Ah

There are an - gels sing - ing no - va can - ti - ca,

Ah

there the bells are ring - ing in re - gis cu - ri - a:

rall.

Ah

O that we were there, O that we were there!

rall.

17
AWAY IN A MANGER

Text: Unknown, Philadelphia (19 *c.*)
Music: Melody by William James Kirkpatrick (1838-1921)
arranged by Malcolm Archer (*b.* 1952)

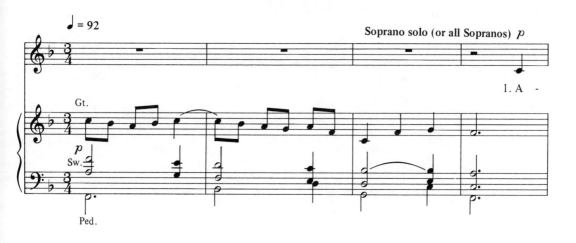

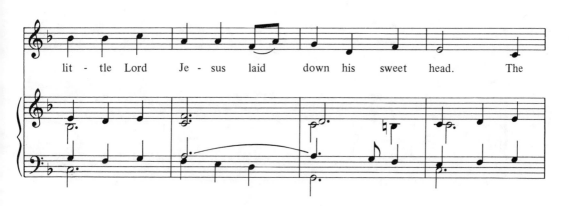

stars in the bright sky looked down where he lay, the

lit - tle Lord Je - sus, a - sleep on the hay.

S
A

2. The cat - tle are low - ing, the ba - by a - wakes, but
3. Be near me, Lord Je - sus, I ask you to stay close

Men

lit - tle Lord Je - sus no cry - ing he makes. I
by me for e - ver, and love me, I pray. Bless

love thee, Lord Je - sus! Look down from the sky, and
all the dear child - ren in thy ten - der care, and

stay by my side un - til morn - ing is nigh.
fit us for hea - ven, to live with thee there.

18

O COME, ALL YE FAITHFUL

Text: Translated from the Latin by Frederick Oakeley (1802-1880)
Music: Melody by John Francis Wade (1711-1786)
arranged by Colin Mawby (b.1936)

1. O come, all ye faith - ful, joy - ful and tri - um - phant, O
3. See how the shep - herds, sum-moned to his cra - dle,

come ye, O come ye to Beth - le - hem;
leav - ing their flocks, draw nigh with low - ly fear;

come and be - hold him born the king of an - gels: O
we too will thi - ther bend our joy - ful foot - steps: O

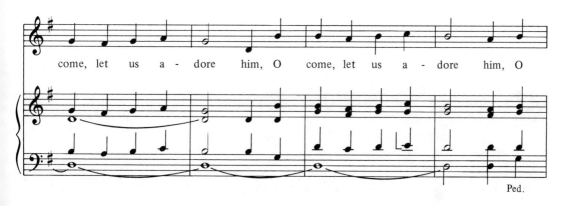

come, let us a - dore him, O come, let us a - dore him, O

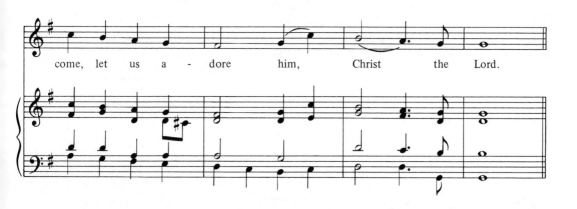

come, let us a - dore him, Christ the Lord.

Descant

2. God of God, Light of Light,
4. Lo, star - led chief - tains, ma - gi, Christ a - dor - ing,

All other voices

2. God of God, Light of Light,
4. Lo, star - led chief - tains, ma - gi, Christ a - dor - ing,

Man.

lo,   he ab - hors   not the   vir - gin's womb;
of - fer him   in - cense,   gold   and myrrh;

lo,   he ab - hors   not the   vir - gin's womb;
of - fer him   in - cense,   gold   and myrrh;

ve - ry   God,   be - got - ten, not cre - a - ted:
we   to the   Christ - child   bring our heart's o - bla - tions:

ve - ry   God,   be - got - ten, not cre - a - ted: O
we   to the   Christ - child   bring our heart's o - bla - tions: O

let   us a - dore   him, O
come, let us a - dore   him, O   come, let us   a - dore   him, O

Ped.

74

D.C.

come, let us a - dore him, Christ the Lord.

come, let us a - dore him, Christ the Lord.

D.C.

5. Child, for us sin - ners poor and in the man - ger, fain we em -

5. Child, for us sin - ners poor and in the man - ger, fain we em -

Man.

brace thee with love and awe; who would not love thee,

brace thee with love and awe; who would not love thee,

loving us so dearly: O come, let us adore him, O come, let us adore him, O come, let us adore him, Christ the Lord.

6. Sing, choirs of angels, sing in exultation, sing, all ye

Unison

Ped.

citi-zens of heav'n a-bove: 'Glo - ry to God in the high - est:' O come, let us a-dore him, O come, let us a-dore him, O come let us a-dore him, Christ the Lord.

Fa - ther, now in flesh ap - pear - ing:

Fa - ther, now in flesh ap - pear - ing: O

come, let us a - dore him, O come, let us a - dore him, O

O

come, Christ the Lord.

come, let us a - dore him, Christ the Lord.

19

For Morwenna

DORMI, JESU

Text: Latin: English paraphrase by Samuel Taylor Coleridge (1772-1834)
Music: Richard Lloyd (*b.* 1933)

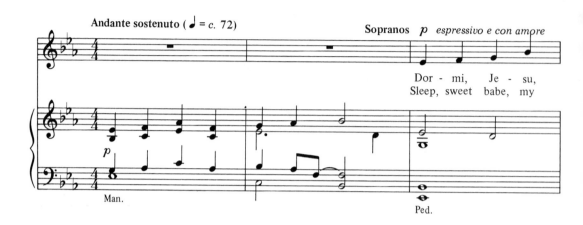

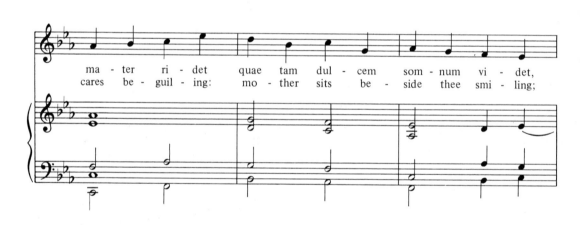

Dormi, Jesu, mater ridet quae tam dulcem somnum videt,
Sleep, sweet babe, my cares beguiling: mother sits beside thee smiling;

dormi, Jesu, blandule.
sleep, my darling, tenderly.

Si non dormis, mater plorat. Inter fila
If thou sleep not, mother mourneth, singing as her

81

can -tans o - rat, blan - de, ve - ni, som -nu - le.
wheel she turn -eth: come, soft slum - ber, balm - i - ly.

S
A

Men

Si   non dor - mis, ma - ter plo - rat.
If   thou sleep not, mo - ther mourn -eth,

dim.

In - ter fi - la can - tans o - rat, blan - de, ve - ni, som - nu-le.
sing -ing as her wheel turn -eth: come, soft slum - ber, bal - mi-ly.

dim.

Sopranos *sostenuto*

Dor - mi, Je - su, ma - ter ri - det quae tam dul - cem

Sleep, sweet babe, my cares be - guil - ing: mo - ther sits be -

som - num vi - det, dor - mi, Je - su,

side thee smil - ing, sleep, my dar - ling,

blan - du - le, dor - mi, blan - du - le.

ten - der - ly, sleep, ten - der - ly.

20
VIRGIN'S SLUMBER SONG

Text: Michael Forster (*b.*1946)
Music: Max Reger (1873-1916) arranged by Richard Lloyd (*b.*1933)

1. O child of hope, what sha-dows fall a-

cross your sleep-ing eyes? Sha-dows of a fu-ture

marked by love and sac - ri - fice;

O child of pro - mise such a cost, but such a prize!

O soft - ly slum - ber,

child   of   grace!

2. Child   of   sor - row, child   of joy,   child   of mys - te -

ry   di - vine,   may your peace-ful, trust - ing sleep   be   of hope the

seal and sign.   O   soft - ly

slum - ber,   child

of   grace!

21
MATER ORA FILIUM

Text: Unknown (15 c.)
Music: Charles Wood (1866-1926), based on an Irish Folk Song
adapted by Christopher Tambling (b. 1964)

Ma - ter o - ra fi - li - um, ut post hoc ex - il - i - um, no - bis do - net

gau - di - um   be - a - to - rum om - ni - um.

mp

1. Fair maid - en, who is   this bairn   that thou bear - est   in thine arm?
2. Man to fa - ther he hath none   but him - self   God a - lone;

mp

mp

D.S. first time only

Sir, it is   a   king - is son,   that in heav'n a - bove doth won.
of   a maid - en he would be born to save man-kind that was for - lorn.

89

Refrain

All voices

Ma-ter o - ra fi - li-um, ut post hoc ex - il - i-um, no - bis do - net

gau - di - um be - a - to-rum om - ni - um.

Men *p*

3. Three kings brought him pre - sents: gold, myrrh and frank - in - cense,

Sopranos and Altos

to my son full of might, king of kings and lord of right.

Refrain

Ma-ter o-ra fi - li-um, ut post hoc ex - il - i - um, no-bis do-net

gau - di - um be - a - to-rum om - ni - um.

All voices

4. Fair maid - en pray for us un - to thy son, sweet Je - sus, that

Ped.

91

he will send us of his grace, in heav'n on high to have a place.

Refrain

Ma-ter o - ra fi - li-um, ut post hoc ex - il - i - um, No-bis do-net

Men

Man.

gau-di - um be - a-to-rum om - ni - um.

Ped.

22

I SAW THREE SHIPS

Text: Traditional English Carol
Music: Traditional English Melody arranged by Malcolm Archer (*b.* 1952)

5. O they sailed in - to Beth - le - hem, On Christ - mas Day, on Christ - mas Day, O they sailed in - to Beth - le - hem, On Christ - mas Day in the morn - ing.

Ah

6. And all the bells on earth shall ring, And
7. And all the angels in heav'n shall sing, On Christ-mas Day, on Christ-mas Day, And
8. And all the souls on earth shall sing, And

simile

Ped.

all the bells on earth shall ring.
all the angels in heav'n shall sing, On Christ - mas Day in the morn - ing.
all the souls on earth shall sing,

On Christ - mas Day, Then

9. Then let us all re - joice a - main! On Christ - mas Day, on Christ - mas Day, Then

marcato

On Christ - mas Day in the morn - ing.

let us all re - joice a - main! On Christ - mas morn - ing

let us all re - joice a - main! On Christ - mas Day in the morn - ing.

95

23

A TENDER SHOOT

Text: William Bartholomew (1793-1867)
Music: Otto Goldschmidt (1829-1907)
arranged by Christopher Tambling (*b.*1964)

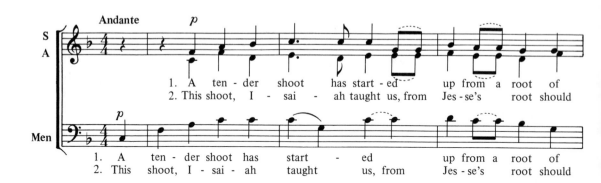

1. A ten - der shoot has start - ed up from a root of
2. This shoot, I - sai - ah taught us, from Jes - se's root should

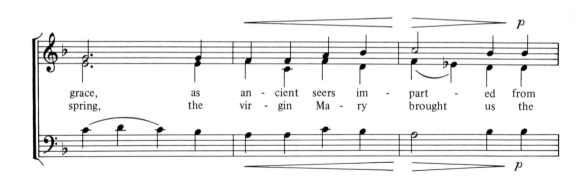

grace, as an - cient seers im - part - ed from
spring, the vir - gin Ma - ry brought us the

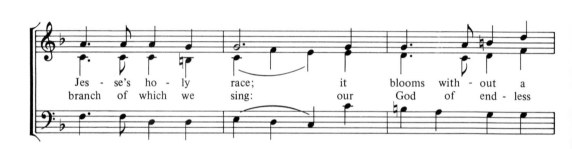

Jes - se's ho - ly race; it blooms with - out a
branch of which we sing: our God of end - less

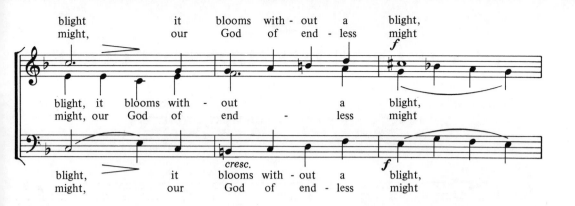

blight   it blooms with - out   a   blight,
might,   our God of end - less might

blight, it blooms with - out   a   blight,
might, our God of end -   less   might

blight,   it   blooms with - out   a   blight,
might,   our   God of end - less   might

blooms in the cold bleak   win -   ter,   turn - ing our
gave her this child to   save   us,   thus   turn - ing

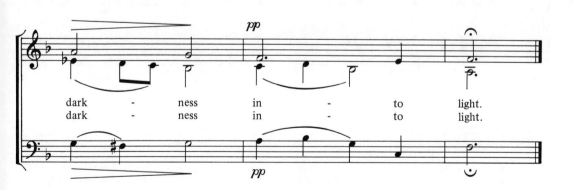

dark -   ness   in -   to   light.
dark -   ness   in -   to   light.

24
IT CAME UPON THE MIDNIGHT CLEAR

Text: Edmund Hamilton Sears (1810-1876)
Music: Traditional English Melody arranged by Arthur Sullivan (1842-1900)
Last verse descant by Malcolm Archer (*b.*1952)

1. It came up-on the mid-night clear, that glo-rious song of
2. Still through the clo-ven skies they come, with peace-ful wings un-
3. Yet with the woes of sin and strife the world has suf-fered

old, from an-gels bend-ing near the earth to touch their harps of
furled; and still their heav'n-ly mu-sic floats o'er all the wea-ry
long; be-neath the an-gel strain have rolled two thou-sand years of

gold; 'Peace on the earth, good-will to men, from heav'n's all-gra-cious
world; a-bove its sad and low-ly plains they bend on hov-'ring
wrong; and man, at war with man, hears not the love-song which they

King!' The world in so-lemn still-ness lay to hear the an-gels sing.
wing; and e-ver o'er its Ba-bel sounds the bless-ed an-gels sing.
bring; O hush the noise, ye men of strife, and hear the an-gels sing!

Descant

4. For lo! the days are haste-ning on, by pro-phet bards fore-

Melody

4. For lo! the days are haste-ning on, by pro-phet bards fore-

told, when with the e - ver - circ - ling years, comes

told, when with the e - ver - circ - ling years, comes

round the age of gold; when peace shall o - ver

round the age of gold; when peace shall o - ver

all the earth its an - cient splen - dours fling, and the whole

all the earth its an - cient splen - dours fling, and

world send back the song which now the an - gels sing.

the whole world give back the song which now the an - gels sing.

25

For Oliver and Teresa Willmott

DING DONG! MERRILY ON HIGH

Text: George Ratcliffe Woodward (1848-1934)
Music: Traditional French Melody (16 c.) arranged by Richard Lloyd (b.1933)

2. E'en so here be-low, be - low, let stee -ple bells be swung - en,

Ding, dong, ding, dong, bells be swung - en,

Ding, dong, ding, dong, bells be swung - en,

and i - o, i - o, i - o, by priest and peo - ple sung - en.

ding, dong, and i - o by priest and peo - ple sung - en.

ding, dong, and i - o by priest and peo - ple sung - en.

3. Pray you, du-ti-ful-ly prime your ma-tin chime, ye ring - ers;

3. Pray you, prime your your ma-tin chime, ye ring-ers;

3. Pray you, prime your your ma-tin chime, ye ring - ers;

may you beau-ti-ful-ly rime your eve-time song, ye sing - ers.

may you rime your song, ye sing - ers.

may you rime your song, ye sing - ers.

107

26
THE GREAT GOD OF HEAVEN

Text: Henry Ramsden Bramley (1833-1917)
Music: Alan Ridout (*b.* 1934)

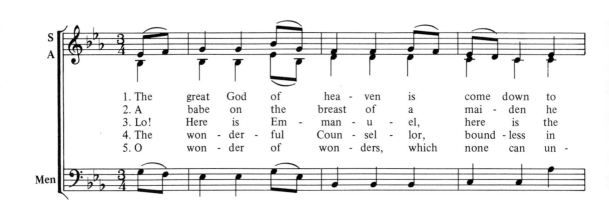

1. The great God of hea - ven is come down to
2. A babe on the breast of a mai - den he
3. Lo! Here is Em - man - u - el, here is the
4. The won - der - ful Coun - sel - lor, bound - less in
5. O won - der of won - ders, which none can un -

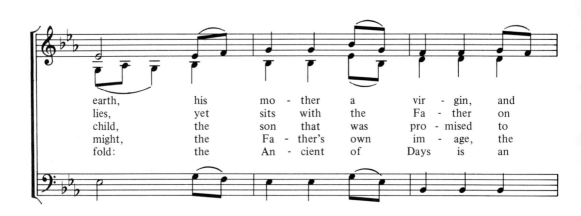

earth, his mo - ther a vir - gin, and
lies, yet sits with the Fa - ther on
child, the son that was pro - mised to
might, the Fa - ther's own im - age, the
fold: the An - cient of Days is an

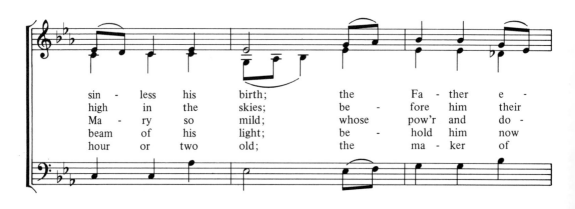

sin - less his birth; the Fa - ther e -
high in the skies; be - fore him their
Ma - ry so mild; whose pow'r and do -
beam of his light; be - hold him now
hour or two old; the ma - ker of

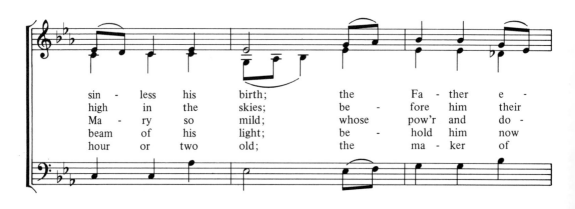

ter - nal his fa - ther a - lone; he
fa - ces the se - ra - phim hide, while
min - ion shall e - ver in - crease, the
wear - ing the like - ness of man; weak,
all things is made of the earth; man is

sleeps in the man - ger, he reigns on the throne.
Jo - seph stands wait - ing, un - scared, by his side.
Prince that shall rule o'er a king - dom of peace.
help - less and speech - less, in mea - sure a span.
wor - shipped by an - gels, and God comes to birth.

Refrain

Then let us a - dore him, and praise his great love: to

save us poor sin - ners he came from a - bove.

27

GOD REST YOU MERRY, GENTLEMEN

Text: Unknown (18 c.)
Music: Traditional English Melody arranged by Colin Mawby (b.1936)

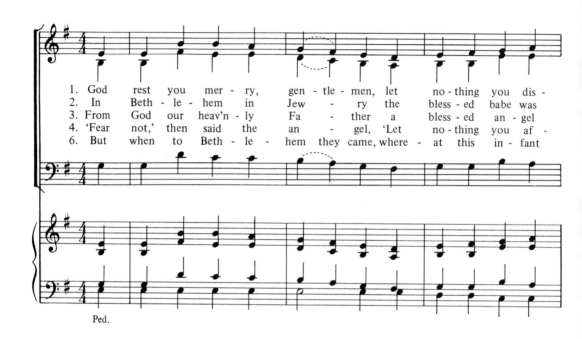

1. God rest you mer - ry, gen - tle - men, let no - thing you dis-
2. In Beth - le - hem in Jew - ry the bless - ed babe was
3. From God our heav'n - ly Fa - ther a bless - ed an - gel
4. 'Fear not,' then said the an - gel, 'Let no - thing you af-
6. But when to Beth - le - hem they came, where - at this in - fant

Ped.

may, for Je - sus Christ our Sa - viour was
born, and laid with - in a man - ger, up-
came, and un - to cer - tain shep - herds brought
fright, this day is born a sa - viour, of
lay, they found him in a man - ger, where

Refrain

born on Christ - mas Day, to save us all from
on this bless - ed morn; to the which his mo - ther
ti - dings of the same, how that in Beth - le -
vir - tue, pow'r and might; so fre - quent - ly to
ox - en feed on hay; his mo - ther Ma - ry

Sa - tan's pow'r when we were gone a - stray:
Ma - ry did no - thing take in scorn:
hem was born the Son of God by name: O
van - quish all the friends of Sa - tan quite:'
kneel - ing, un - to the Lord did pray:

ti - dings of com - fort and joy, com-fort and

111

D.C. for verses 2, 3, 4

joy, O ti - dings of com - fort and joy.

Descant

Re - joi - ced much in

All other voices

5. The shep - herds at those ti - dings re - joi - ced much in

mind, and left their flocks a - feed - ing, in tem - pest, storm and

mind, and left their flocks a - feed - ing, in tem - pest, storm and

112

wind, to Beth - le - hem straight-way this bless - ed babe to

wind, and went to Beth - le - hem straight-way this bless - ed babe to

find: O ti - dings of com - fort and joy, com-fort and

find: O ti - dings of com - fort and joy, com-fort and

D.C. for verse 6

joy. O ti - dings of com - fort and joy.

joy. O ti - dings of com - fort and joy.

Unison

7. Now to the Lord sing prai - ses, all you with-in this place, and with true love and bro-ther-hood each o - ther now em - brace; this ho -ly tide of Christ - mas all o -thers doth de - face: O ti - dings of com - fort and joy, com-fort and joy, O ti - dings of com - fort and joy.

28
I WONDER AS I WANDER

Text: Traditional North American Carol
Music: Traditional North American Melody arranged by Noel Rawsthorne (*b.* 1929)

Sopranos *mp*

un - der the sky.

2. When

Man.

Ma - ry birth'd Je - sus, 'twas in a cow's stall with wise men and farm - ers and

shep - herds and all. But high from God's hea - ven a star's light did fall, and the

pro - mise of a - ges it did then re - call.

mf Gt. *legato*

Ped.

Descant

mf

3. If Je - sus had want - ed for a - ny wee thing, a

All other voices

mf

star in the sky, or a bird on the wing, or all of God's an - gels in

heav'n for to sing, he sure - ly could have it, 'cause he was the king.

f *rall.*

f *rall.*

rall.

117

29

HARK, THE HERALD ANGELS SING

Text: Charles Wesley (1707-1788), George Whitefield (1714-1770),
Martin Madan (1726-1790) and others
Music: Felix Mendelssohn (1809-1847)
last verse arrangement Colin Mawby (b.1936)

1. Hark, the he- rald an- gels sing glo- ry to the new-born king; peace on earth and
2. Christ, by high- est heav'n a- dored Christ, the e- ver- last- ing Lord; late in time be-

Ped.

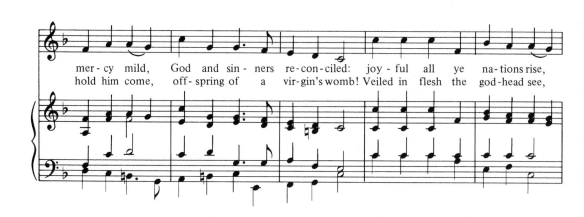

mer- cy mild, God and sin- ners re- con- ciled: joy- ful all ye na- tions rise,
hold him come, off- spring of a vir- gin's womb! Veiled in flesh the god- head see,

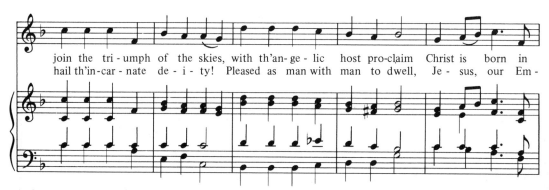

join the tri- umph of the skies, with th'an- ge- lic host pro- claim Christ is born in
hail th'in- car- nate de- i- ty! Pleased as man with man to dwell, Je- sus, our Em-

* If sung in harmony, follow the accompaniment with the men taking the tenor line.

Beth-le-hem. Hark, the her-ald an-gels sing glo-ry to the new-born king.
man-u - el. Hark, the her-ald an-gels sing glo-ry to the new-born king.

new-born king.

very rhythmical

Man.

Descant

3. Hail the heav'n - born prince of peace!

All other voices

3. Hail the heav'n - born prince of peace!

Ped.

Hail the sun of right - eous - ness! Light and life to
all he brings, ri - sen with heal - ing in his wings;
mild he lays his glo - ry by, born that man no

more may die, born to raise the sons of earth,

more may die, born to raise the sons of earth,

born to give them se - cond birth. Hark, the he - rald

born to give them se - cond birth. Hark, the he - rald

an - gels sing glo - ry to the new - born king.

an - gels sing glo - ry to the new - born king.

30

LULLAY MY LIKING

Text: From the *Sloane* Manuscript (*c.*15 *c.*)
Music: Gustav Holst (1874-1934) arranged by Alan Ridout (*b.* 1934)

3. There was mick - le me - lo - dy at that child - es birth: al - though

To Refrain

they were in hea - ven's bliss they ma - de mick - le mirth.

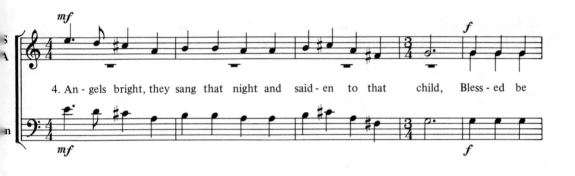

4. An - gels bright, they sang that night and said - en to that child, Bless - ed be

To Refrain

thou, and so be she, that is both meek and mild.'

To Refrain

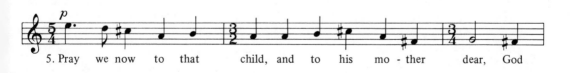

5. Pray we now to that child, and to his mo - ther dear, God

To Refrain

grant them all his bless - ing that now ma - ken cheer.

mickle = much

31
For Maria
TYROLEAN CAROL

Text: Harrison Oxley (*b.*1933)
Music: Traditional Tyrolean melody arranged by Harrison Oxley

* It preferred, the altos and men could remain silent for v.1, or the altos could sing with sopranos with men silent.

† short 'a'

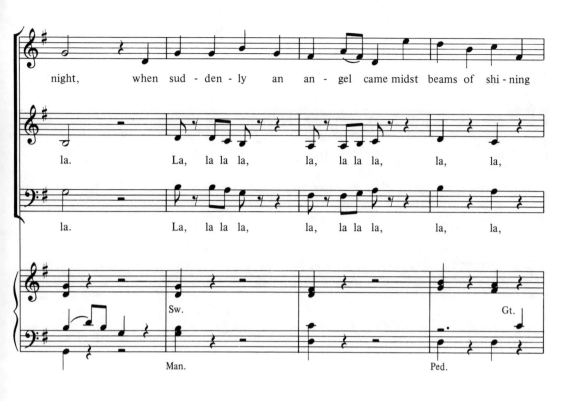

night, when sud-den-ly an an-gel came midst beams of shi-ning

la. La, la la la, la, la la la, la, la,

la. La, la la la, la, la la la, la, la,

Sw. Gt.

Man. Ped.

light. 'A-wake, you la-zy shep-herd men' God's mes-sen-ger did

la. La, la, la, la, la, la,

la. La, la, la, la, la, la,

Sw. Gt.

say: 'to-day is Christ the Sa - viour born, to Beth-lem make your

la. la, la la la, la, la la la, la, la,

la. la, la la la, la, la la la, la, la,

way!' 2. And

la.

la.

lo, a won-drous heav'n-ly host filled all the star-ry sky. The

La, la la la, la, la la la, la, la, la.

La, la la la, la, la la la, la, la, la.

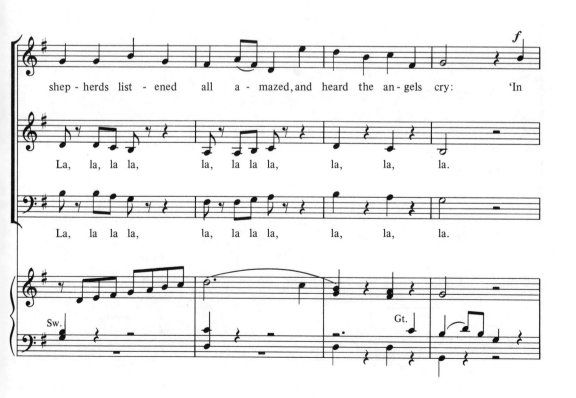

shep - herds list - ened all a - mazed, and heard the an - gels cry: 'In

La, la, la la, la, la la la, la, la, la.

La, la la la, la, la la la, la, la, la.

high - est heav'n now glo - ry be for Je - sus' ho - ly birth; good

La, la, la, la, la, la, la.

La, la, la, la, la, la, la.

(Gt.)

Sw.

news we bring to all the world and peace to men on earth.'

La, la, la la, la, la la la, la, la, la.

La, la la la, la, la la la, la, la, la.

Gt.

A few Sopranos (Optional Descant)

Most Sopranos, and Altos

f

3. So

Men

f

3. So

Sing glo - ry, glo - ry, praise Je - sus'

'Glo - ry be to God the Lord' let all man - kind pro -

'Glo - ry be to God the Lord' let all man - kind pro -

Gt.

Sw.

f

Gt.

129

name! Sing glo - ry, glo - ry, praise Je - sus'

claim; sing glo - ry with the an - gel host to Je - sus' ho - ly

claim; sing glo - ry with the an - gel host to Je - sus' ho - ly

Sw. Gt.

name! Glo - ry to God!

name! Most joy - ful - ly this Christ - mas - tide our

name! Glo - ry to God!

(Gt.)

Sw.

Glo - ry to God! Sing

praise and love we bring: sing glo - ry, glo - ry,

Glo - ry to God! Sing glo - ry, glo - ry,

glo - ry, glo - ry, praise to Christ our King!

glo - ry now to Christ our new - born King!

glo - ry now to Christ our new - born King!

32

SLEEP, MY LITTLE BABE, SLEEP

Text: Luke Connaughton (1919-1979)
Music: John Googe (*b*.1942) arranged by Stanley Vann (*b*.1910)

* Dynamics of accompaniment to suit those of the singers.

Refrain

So lull the ba-by,

news that breathed of spring.
side the in - fant king.
death has lost its sting!
bove each mor - tal thing.

So lull the ba - by,

sing him to sleep.   Sleep, my lit - tle babe, sleep

sing him to sleep.   Sleep, my lit - tle babe, sleep.

33

CHRISTMAS FOR GOD'S HOLY PEOPLE

Text: Michael Saward (b.1932)
Music: Sydney Carter (b.1915) arranged by Norman Warren (b.1934)

1. Christ-mas for God's ho-ly peo-ple is a time of joy and peace: so, all christ-ian men and wo-men,
2. Child of Ma-ry, vir-gin mo-ther, pea-sant ba-by yet our King, cra-dled there a-mong the ox-en:

hymns and ca - rols let us raise to our God
joy - ful ca - rols now we sing to our God

come to earth, Son of Man by hu - man birth.
come to earth, Son of Man by hu - man birth.

Sopranos (or solo) *mp*

3. An - gel ar - mies

mp

Man.

135

sang in cho-rus at our Christ's na - ti - vi - ty, he who came to share our na-ture: so we sing with gai - e - ty to our God come to earth, Son of Man by hu - man birth.

Men

4. Shep-herds hur - ried to the man-ger, saw the babe in Beth-le - hem,

Ped.

glo - ri -fied the God of hea - ven: now we join to sing with them

to our God come to earth, Son of Man by hu - man birth.

137

5. In-fant low-ly, born in squa-lor, pro-phet, king and great high priest,

Word of God, to us des-cend-ing: still we sing both great and least,

to our God come to earth, Son of Man by hu-man birth.

to our God come to earth, Son of Man by hu-man birth.

34
LITTLE JESUS, SWEETLY SLEEP

Text: Traditional Czech Carol translated by Percy Dearmer (1867-1936)
Music: Traditional Czech Melody arranged by Alan Ridout (b.1934)

Ah

Ah

we will lend a coat of fur; we will rock you,
sleep in com - fort, slum - ber deep; we will rock you,

Ah

mp

rock you, rock you, we will rock you, rock you, rock you:
rock you, rock you, we will rock you, rock you, rock you:

Ah

Ah

see the fur to keep you warm, snug - ly round your
we will serve you all we can, dar - ling, dar - ling

Fine

D.S. al Fine

ti - ny form.
lit - tle man.

Fine

D.S. al Fine

35

CHRIST WAS BORN ON CHRISTMAS DAY

Text: John Mason Neale (1818-1866)
Music: Melody from *Piae Cantiones* (1582) arranged by Colin Mawby (*b.*1936)

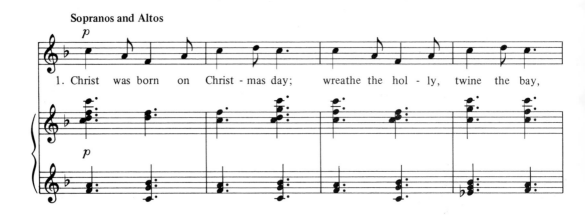

1. Christ was born on Christ-mas day; wreathe the hol - ly, twine the bay,

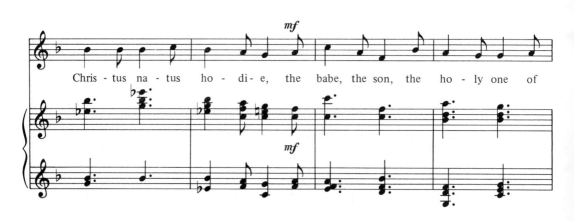

Chris - tus na - tus ho - di - e, the babe, the son, the ho - ly one of

Ma - ry. Chris - tus na - tus ho - di - e.

2. He is born to

set us free; he is born our Lord to be, ex Ma - ri - a

vir - gi - ne, the God, the Lord, a - dored by all for e - ver.

Sopranos

3. Let the bright red ber - ries glow

143

ev - 'ry-where in good - ly show, Chris - tus na - tus ho - di - e, the

babe, the son, the ho - ly one of Ma - ry.

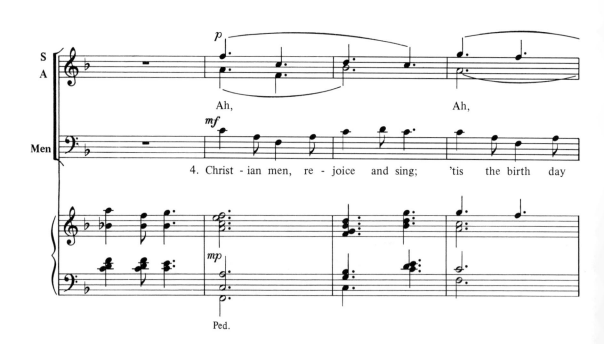

S
A

Ah,   Ah,

Men

4. Christ - ian men, re - joice and sing; 'tis the birth day

mf

mp

Ped.

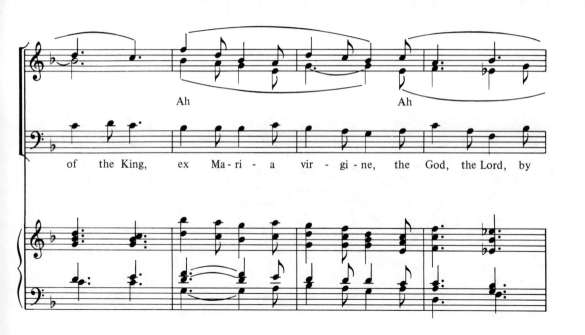

Ah   Ah

of the King, ex Ma - ri - a vir - gi - ne, the God, the Lord, by

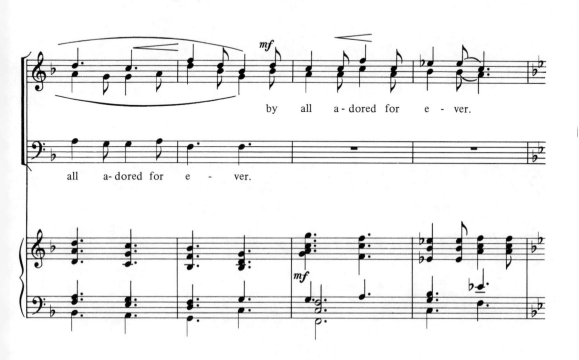

by all a - dored for e - ver.

all a - dored for e - ver.

Unison

5. Night of sad-ness, morn of glad-ness e - ver-more; e - ver,

Man.

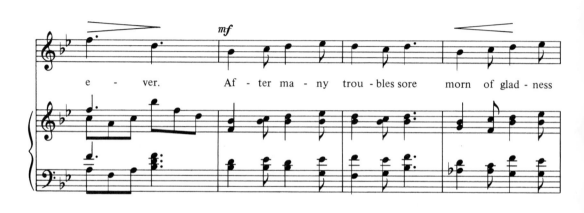

e - ver. Af - ter ma - ny trou-bles sore morn of glad - ness

e - ver-more and e - ver-more.

Sopranos

Mid - night scarce - ly past and o - ver, draw - ing to this

ho - ly morn; ve - ry ear - ly, ve - ry ear - ly Christ was born.

Christ was born on Christ-mas day, Chris - tus na - tus ho - di - e.

Mid - night scarce - ly past and o - ver

36

RISE UP NOW, YE SHEPHERDS

Text: Unknown (possibly from the French)
Music: Alan Ridout (*b.*1934)

1. Rise up now, ye shep-herds, haste with joy to greet the morn on which our bless-ed Sa-viour, Christ the Lord, is born.
2. Now in Da-vid's ci-ty born, of Da-vid's roy-al line, is he who saves from dark-ness those in sin that pine.
3. Hail, O sa-cred in-fant, gen-tle, lov-ing, mild and sweet; our sov-reign Lord and Sa-viour, Christ the Lord, we greet.
4. Hail, O day-star light-ing those in sha-dow and in pain; our hearts' true hope and trea-sure, bliss and joy and gain.
5. Bliss-ful-ly we praise thee, mak-ing now these walls re-sound with tid-ings of sal-va-tion to all men a-round.

Refrain

f Glo-ry in the high-est, (*ff* last time)

peace on earth we sing, for to-day is born a Sa-viour: Christ the Lord is King.

37

MY DANCING DAY

Text: Traditional English Carol
Music: Traditional English Melody arranged by Richard Lloyd (*b.* 1933)

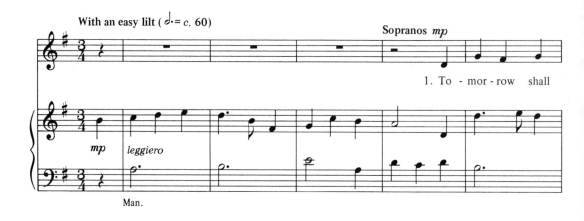

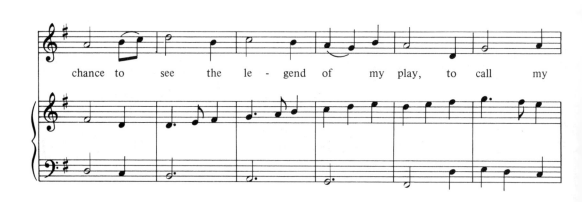

true love to my dance: sing O my love, O my

love, my love, my love, this have I done for my true

love.   2. Then

                                    of a

was I born of a vir - gin pure, of her I

151

took flesh - ly sub - stance; thus was I knit to man's na -

cresc.

Refrain
mf

ture, to call my true love to my dance: sing O my

cresc.

mf

love, O my love, my love, my love; this have I

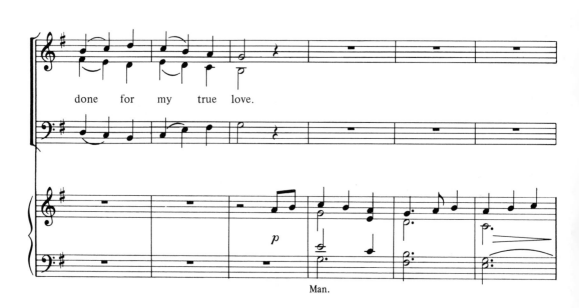

done for my true love.

p

Man.

3. In a man - ger laid and wrapped I was, so ve - ry poor, this was my chance, be - twixt an ox and a sil - ly poor ass, to call my true love to my dance: sing O my love, O my love, my love, my love; this have I

hum

Refrain

love, O my love, my love, my love, my love; this have I
sing O my love, sing O my love, my love; have I

153

done for my true love.

done for my true love.

mp *cresc.*

Man.

Descant

4. Sing O my love, O my love, O my

All other voices

4. To - mor-row shall be my danc - ing day: I would my

f

Ped.

love this have I done for my true

true love did so chance to see the le - gend of my

Refrain

love,   for my   true   love;   sing

play,   to call   my   true   love   to   my   dance; sing   O   my

sing,   O   my   love,   sing   O   my   love,

love,   O   my   love,   my   love,   my   love; this   have   I   done   for

molto allarg.

O   my   love;   this   have   I   done   for   my   true   love.

my   true   love;   this   have   I   done   for   my   true   love.

molto allarg.

38
RISE UP, SHEPHERD, AND FOLLOW

Text and Music: American Spiritual
arranged by Malcolm Archer (*b.* 1952)

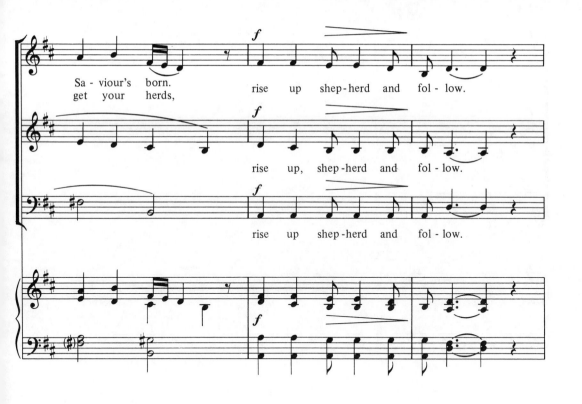

Sa - viour's born.
get your herds,

rise up shep-herd and fol - low.

rise up, shep-herd and fol - low.

rise up shep-herd and fol - low.

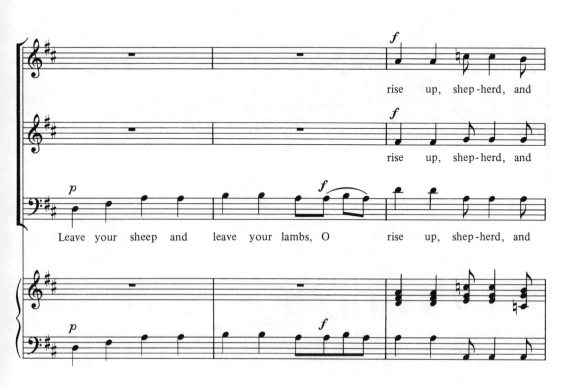

rise up, shep-herd, and

rise up, shep-herd, and

Leave your sheep and leave your lambs, O rise up, shep-herd, and

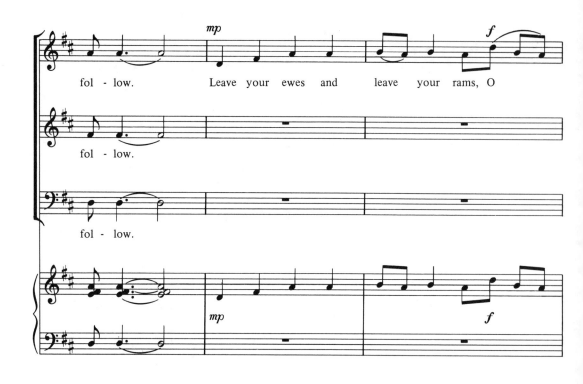

fol - low.   Leave your ewes and   leave   your   rams, O

fol - low.

fol - low.

rise   up, shep-herd, and   fol - low.   Fol -   low,   fol - low,

rise   up, shep-herd, and   fol - low.   Fol -   low,   fol - low,

rise   up, shep-herd, and   fol - low.   Fol -   low,   fol - low,

rise up, shep-herd, and fol-low. Fol-low the star of

rise up, shep-herd, and fol-low. oo

rise up, shep-herd, and fol-low. oo

Beth - le - hem, Rise up, shep-herd, and fol-low.

Rise up, shep-herd, and fol-low.

Rise up, shep-herd, and fol-low.

Ped.

Man.

39

For the Durham Cathedral Choristers

IN THE BLEAK MID-WINTER

Text: Christina Rossetti (1830-1894)
Music: Richard Lloyd (b.1933)

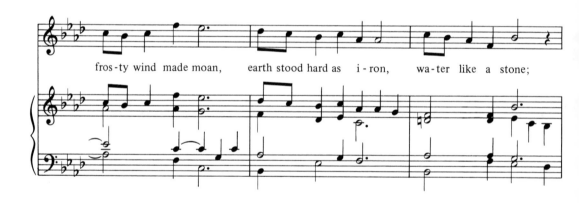

long a - go.

Man.

2. Our God, heav'n can - not hold him, nor earth sus - tain;

ten.

a tempo

ten.

a tempo

Ped.

heav'n and earth shall flee a - way when he comes to reign:

40
IN THE BLEAK MID-WINTER

Text: Christina Rossetti (1830-1894)
Music: Gustav Holst (1874-1934) arranged by Harrison Oxley (b.1933)

* Verse 2 may be sung by men (melody line), sopranos and altos remaining silent.

i - ron, wa - ter like a stone; snow had fall - en,
flee a - way when he comes to reign: in the bleak mid -
se - ra - phim thronged the air: but on - ly his

snow on snow, snow on snow,
win - ter a sta - ble place suf - ficed the
mo - ther in her mai - den bliss

Repeat for verse 2

in the bleak mid - win - ter, long a - go.
Lord God al - might - y, Je - sus Christ.
wor - shipped the be - lov - ed with a kiss.

165

Sopranos and Altos

3. E - nough for him, whom che - ru - bim wor - ship night and day, a breast - ful of milk and a man - ger - ful of hay; e - nough for him, whom an - gels fall down be - fore, the

41

WHEN GOD WAS MINDED TO BE BORN

Text: Mark Woodruff (*b.* 1952)
Music: Traditional English Melody arranged by Malcolm Archer (*b.* 1952)

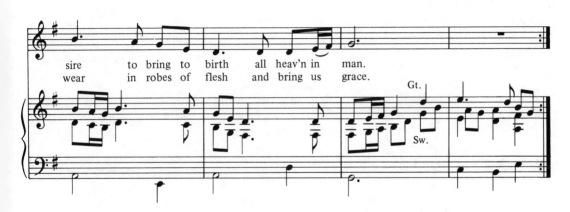

3. Now in the full - ness of his time, when all the world its si - lence keeps, the Word of God's re - deem -ing love to Ma - ry's womb from hea - ven leaps.

4. Shep-herds and

Ah

kings,   do you not   see?   Be - hold your God's   hu - mi - li -

ty;   who'd waive such   bliss   for mor - tal   birth,   to swathe us   in   di - vi - ni -

ty!

42

UNTO US IS BORN A SON

Text: Latin (15 c.) translated by George Ratcliffe Woodward (1848-1934)
Music: Melody from *Piae Cantiones* (1582) arranged by Malcolm Archer (*b.* 1952)

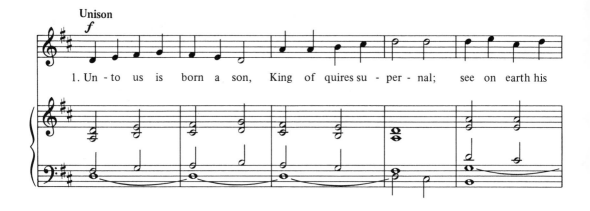

1. Un - to us is born a son, King of quires su - per - nal; see on earth his

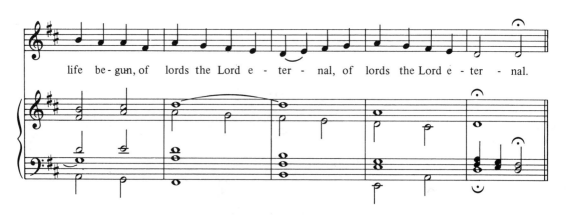

life be - gun, of lords the Lord e - ter - nal, of lords the Lord e - ter - nal.

Sopranos

2. Christ, from heav'n des - cend -ing low, comes on earth a stran -ger: ox and ass their own -er know, be - cra - dled in the man - ger, be cra - dled in the man - ger.

Men

3. This did He- rod sore af -fray, and grie -vous- ly be - wild - er, so he gave the word to slay, and slew the lit - tle child - er, and slew the lit - tle child - er.

4. Of his love and mer - cy mild this the Christ - mas sto - ry, and O that Ma - ry's gen - tle child might lead us up to glo - ry, might lead us up to glo - ry!

Descant *f*

Ah

All other voices *f*

5. 'O' and 'A', and 'A' and 'O' cum can - ti - bus in cho - ro;

Sw.

f Gt.

Ped.

Ah

let the mer - ry or - gan go, Be - ne - di - ca - mus

Ah

rall.

Do - mi - no, Be - ne - di - ca - mus Do - mi - no.

rall.

175

43

INFANT HOLY, INFANT LOWLY

Text: Polish Carol translated by Edith Margaret Gellibrand Reed (1885-1933)
Music: Traditional Polish Melody arranged by Malcolm Archer (*b.* 1952)

1. In - fant ho - ly, in - fant low - ly, for his bed a cat - tle
2. Flocks were sleep - ing, shep - herds keep - ing vi - gil till the morn - ing

stall; ox - en low - ing, lit - tle know - ing Christ the
new; saw the glo - ry, heard the sto - ry, tid - ings

babe is Lord of all. Swift are wing - ing an - gels
of a gos - pel true. Thus re - joic - ing, free from

sing - ing, no - wells ring - ing, tid - ings bring - ing, Christ the
sor - row, prai - ses voic - ing, greet the mor - row, Christ the

babe is Lord of all, Christ the babe is Lord of all.
babe was born for you! Christ the babe was born for you!

44

THE SANS DAY CAROL

Text: Collected by Percy Dearmer (1867-1936)
Music: Traditional Cornish Melody arranged by Malcolm Archer (*b.* 1952)

1. Now the hol - ly bears a ber - ry as white as the
hol - ly bears a ber - ry as green as the

milk, and Ma - ry bore Je - sus, who was wrapped up in
grass, and Ma - ry bore Je - sus, who died on the

2. Now the

3. Now the

Sw.

hol - ly bears a ber - ry as black as the coal, and

Ma - ry bore Je - sus, who died for us all: and

Ma - ry bore Je -sus Christ our Sa - viour for to be, and the

first tree in the green-wood, it was the hol - ly, hol - ly, hol -

ly, and the first tree in the green - wood, it was the hol -

ly!

Gt.

Sw.
mp

Ped.

All *mf*

4. Now the hol - ly bears a ber - ry, as blood it is

Sw. *mf*

red, and trust we our Sa - viour, who rose from the

cresc. *f*

dead: and Ma - ry bore Je - sus Christ our

mp

Sa - viour for to be, and the first tree in the green - wood, it

was the hol - ly, hol - ly hol - ly, and the

first tree in the green - wood, it was the hol - ly!

45
IN A CAVERN OXEN TROD

Text: Translated from the Dutch by George Ratcliffe Woodward (1848-1934)
Music: Stanley Vann (b.1910)

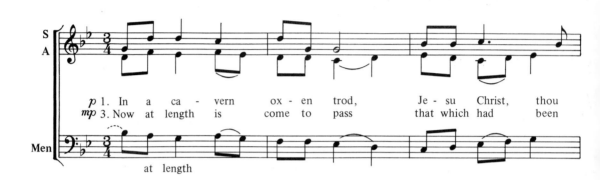

p 1. In a ca - vern ox - en trod, Je - su Christ, thou
mp 3. Now at length is come to pass that which had been

at length

li - est in a man - ger, ve - ry God,
told - en touch - ing Christ and Christ - en - mass,

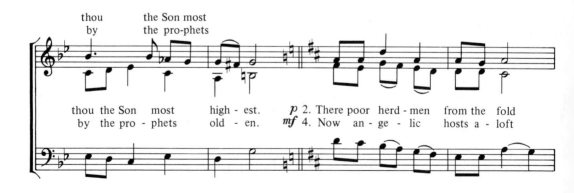

thou   the Son most
by   the pro-phets

thou the Son   most   high - est.   p 2. There poor herd - men   from the   fold
by the pro - phets   old - en.   mf 4. Now an - ge - lic   hosts a - loft

there   with in - cense
ca   rol -ling, in

bend the knee   be -   fore   thee: there with in - cense,
cleave the sky   a -   sun - der,   ca - rol - ling, in

poco rit.   *D.C. for verse 3*

myrrh and gold,   east -   ern   kings a - dore thee.
loud and soft,   songs   of   glee and won - der.

a - dore thee. *mp* 3. Now
and   won - der. *f* 5. Glo -

f 5. 'Glo-ry be to   God,' they cry,   'God who con - de - scend - est

- ry be

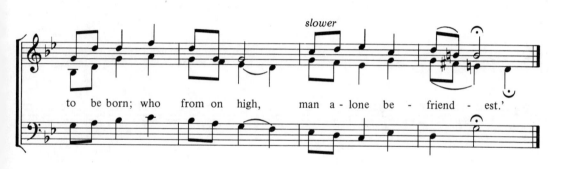

slower

to be born; who from on high,   man a - lone be - friend - est.'

46

MARY HAD A BABY

Text and Music: West Indian Traditional
arranged by Malcolm Archer (*b.* 1952)

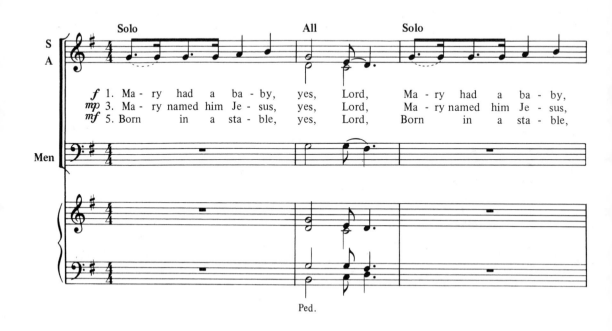

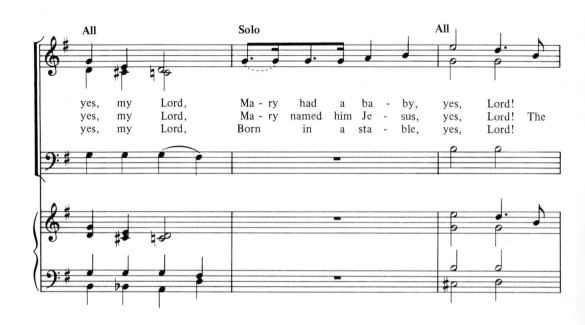

peo - ple keep a com-ing, but the train has gone! **_mp_** 2. What did she name him,
_mp_ 4. Where was he born,
_p_ 6. Where did she lay him,

Solo

yes, Lord, what did she name him, yes, my Lord,
yes, Lord, where was he born, yes, my Lord,
yes, Lord, where did she lay him, yes, my Lord,

Solo

Man.

All

What did she name him, yes, Lord?
Where was he born, yes, Lord? Ah
Where did she lay him,

Solo

The peo - ple keep a com-ing but the

7. Laid him in a man - ger, yes, Lord,

train has gone!

Laid him in a man - ger, yes, my Lord, Laid him in a man - ger,

yes, Lord! The peo - ple keep a com-ing but the train has gone!

47

WHILE SHEPHERDS WATCHED THEIR FLOCKS

Text: Nahum Tate (1652-1715)
Music: From Thomas Este's *Psalmes* (1592) arranged by Harrison Oxley (*b.*1933)

1. While shep - herds watched their flocks by night, all

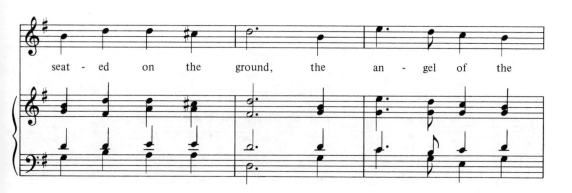

seat - ed on the ground, the an - gel of the

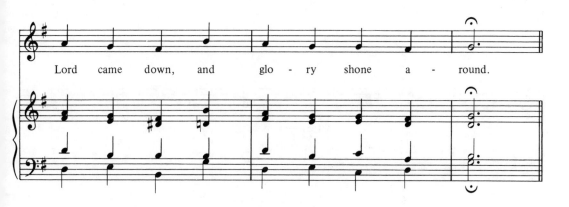

Lord came down, and glo - ry shone a - round.

2. 'Fear not,' said he, (for migh - ty dread had
3. To you, in Da - vid's town this day is
4. The heav'n - ly babe you there shall find to
5. Thus spake the ser - aph, and forth - with ap -

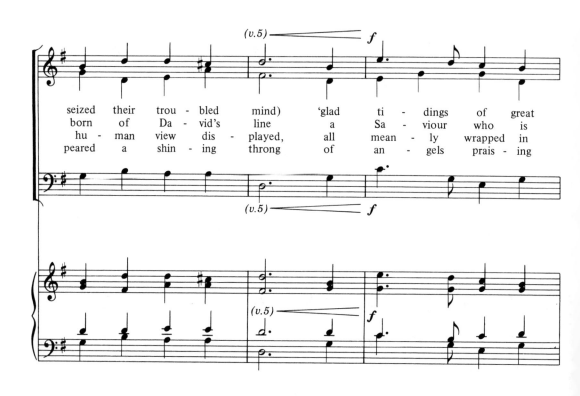

seized their trou - bled mind) 'glad ti - dings of great
born of Da - vid's line a Sa - viour who is
hu - man view dis - played, all mean - ly wrapped in
peared a shin - ing throng of an - gels prais - ing

(v.5)

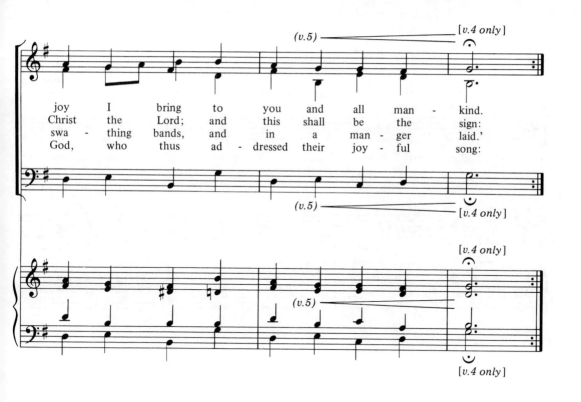

joy I bring to you and all man - kind.
Christ the Lord; and this shall be the sign:
swa - thing bands, and in a man - ger laid.'
God, who thus ad - dressed their joy - ful song:

(v.5) ———————— [v.4 only]

Descant

ff

6. 'All glo - ry be to God on high, and

All other voices

ff

6. 'All glo - ry be to God on high, and

191

on the earth be peace; good-will hence-forth from

on the earth be peace; good - will hence-forth from

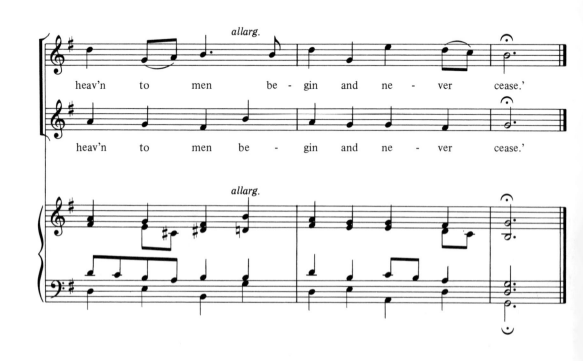

heav'n to men be - gin and ne - ver cease.'

heav'n to men be - gin and ne - ver cease.'

48

SING LULLABY

Text: Sabine Baring-Gould (1834-1924)
Music: Old Basque Noël arranged by Philip Moore (*b*.1943)

clin - ing, sing lul - la - by! Hush, do not wake the in - fant
sleep - ing, sing lul - la - by! Hush, do not wake the in - fant
doz - ing, sing lul - la - by! Hush, do not wake the in - fant
wa - king, sing lul - la - by! Hush, do not wake the in - fant

clin - ing, sing lul - la - by! Hush, do not wake the in - fant
sleep - ing, sing lul - la - by! Hush, do not wake the in - fant
doz - ing, sing lul - la - by! Hush, do not wake the in - fant
wa - king, sing lul - la - by! Hush, do not wake the in - fant

clin - ing, sing lul - la - by! Hush, do not wake the
sleep - ing, sing lul - la - by! Hush, do not wake the
doz - ing, sing lul - la - by! Hush, do not wake the
wa - king, sing lul - la - by! Hush, do not wake the

king; an - gels are watch - ing, stars are shin - ing o - ver the
king; soon will come sor - row with the morn - ing, soon will come
king; soon comes the cross, the nails, the pierc - ing, then in the
king; dream - ing of Eas - ter, joy - ful morn - ing, con-quer-ing

king; an - gels are watch - ing, stars are shin - ing o - ver the
king; soon will come sor - row with the morn - ing, soon will come
king; soon comes the cross, the nails, the pierc - ing, then in the
king; dream - ing of Eas - ter, joy - ful morn - ing, con-quer-ing

king; an - gels are watch - ing, stars are shin - ing o - ver the
king; soon will come sor - row with the morn - ing, soon will come
king; soon comes the cross, the nails, the pierc - ing, then in the
king; dream - ing of Eas - ter, joy - ful morn - ing, con-quer-ing

194

place where he is ly - ing: sing lul - la - by!
bit - ter grief and weep - ing: sing lul - la - by!
grave at last re - pos - ing: sing lul - la - by!
death, its bond - age break - ing; sing lul - la - by!

place where he is ly - ing: sing lul - la - by!
bit - ter grief and weep - ing: sing lul - la - by!
grave at last re - pos - ing: sing lul - la - by!
death, its bond - age break - ing: sing lul - la - by!

place where he is ly - ing: sing lul - la - by!
bit - ter grief and weep - ing: sing lul - la - by!
grave at last re - pos - ing: sing lul - la - by!
death, its bond - age break - ing: sing lul - la - by!

49

GLORY'S DAWN

Text: Mark Woodruff (*b.*1959)
Music: Melody from *Piae Cantiones* (1582), arranged by Richard Lloyd (*b.*1933)

1. When our Lord's lov - ing mind

thought to save lost man - kind, on - ly one could he find

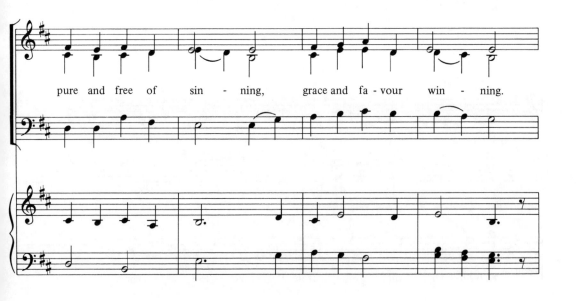

pure and free of sin - ning, grace and fa - vour win - ning.

Refrain

mf

O the night is day: sin is turned a - way!

mf

Glo - ry's dawn: Love is born, Je - sus Christ our Sa - viour.

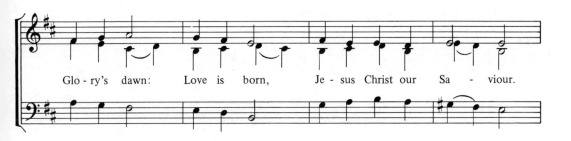

Men *mf*

2. For in God's cho-sen time Ma-ry saw

mf

Ped.

heav'n sub-lime light a way from the crime Eve and A-dam's thiev - ing

did to true be - liev - ing.

Refrain
f

O the night is day: sin is turned

f

a - way! Glo-ry's dawn: Love is born, Je - sus Christ our Sa - viour.

Sopranos and Altos

mp

3. What may tell more of grace

Man.

than this pure mo-ther's face, shin-ing clear on our race,

Light of Light re - flect - ing, God of God pro - tect - ing?

Refrain

mf

O the night is day: sin is turned a - way!

Glo - ry's dawn: Love is born, Je - sus Christ our Sa - viour.

S
A

Men

mf

4. Wrong and ill shall be right

mf

Ped.

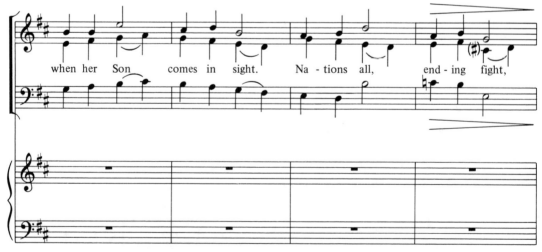

when her Son comes in sight. Na - tions all, end - ing fight,

bowed in peace be - fore him, will, like her, a - dore him.

poco allarg.

poco allarg.

mf

Man.

Refrain
Descant
ff poco meno mosso

O the night is day: sin is turned a - way!

Melody
ff

O the night is day: sin is turned a - way!

poco meno mosso

ff

Ped.

molto rall.

Glo - ry's dawn: Love is born, our Sa - viour.

Glo - ry's dawn: Love is born, Je - sus Christ our Sa - viour.

molto rall.

50
RIGHTEOUS JOSEPH

Text: Traditional Cornish Carol
Music: Alan Ridout (b. 1934)

1. When right - eous Jo - seph wed - ded was to Is - rael's
2. Thus Ma - ry and her hus - band kind to - ge - ther
3. Sing prai - ses all, both young and old, to him that

He - brew maid, the an - gel Ga - briel
did re - main un - til the time of
wrought such things; and all with - out the

came from heav'n, and to the vir - gin said:
Je - sus' birth, as scrip - ture doth make plain.
means of man, sent us the King of kings,

'Hail, bless - ed Ma - ry, full of grace, the
As mo - ther, wife and vir - tuous maid our
who is of such a spi - rit blest that

Lord re - main on thee; thou shalt con - ceive and
Sa - viour sweet con - ceived; and in due time to
with his might did quell the world, the flesh, and

bear a son our Sa - viour for to be.'
bring us him, of whom we were be - reaved.
by his death did con - quer death and hell.

Refrain

Then sing you all, both great and small, no - well, no -

well, no - well! We may re - joice to hear the

voice of the an - gel Ga - bri - el.

51

HAIL, BLESSED VIRGIN MARY!

Text: George Ratcliffe Woodward (1848-1934) (adapted)
Music: Italian, arranged by Harrison Oxley (b.1933)

might - y Ga - bri - el: and thus we greet thee. Come
an - gel - us shall ring from ev - 'ry stee - ple, to

might - y Ga - bri - el: and thus we greet thee. Come
an - gel - us shall ring from ev - 'ry stee - ple, to

might - y Ga - bri - el: and thus we greet thee. Come
an - gel - us shall ring from ev - 'ry stee - ple, to

weal, come woe, our hymn shall ne - ver va - ry:
sound his vir - gin - birth, Al - le - lu - i - a! 2. A - ve, a - ve Ma-

weal, come woe, our hymn shall ne - ver va - ry:
sound his vir - gin - birth, Al - le - lu - i - a!

weal, come woe, our hymn shall ne - ver va - ry:
sound his vir - gin - birth, Al - le - lu - i - a! 1. Hail, bless - ed vir - gin

Hail, bless-ed vir-gin Ma - ry!
ri - a! A - ve, a - ve Ma - ri - a!

Hail, bless-ed vir-gin Ma - ry!
A - ve, a - ve Ma - ri - a!

Ma ry! Hail, bless-ed vir-gin Ma - ry!
A - ve, a - ve Ma - ri - a!

3. Arch - an - gels chant 'Ho - san - na!' and

and

3. Arch - an - gels chant 'Ho - san - na!'

Man. Ped.

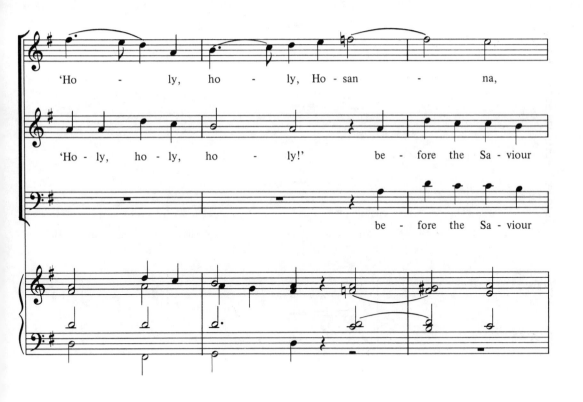

'Ho - ly, ho - ly, Ho - san - na,

'Ho - ly, ho - ly, ho - ly!' be - fore the Sa - viour

be - fore the Sa - viour

Ho - san - na, Ho - san - na! the Light pro - claimed by

born of mai - den low - ly, the Light pro - claimed by

born of mai - den low - ly, the Light pro - claimed by

Si - me - on and An - na.   Arch - an - gels

Si - me - on and An - na.

Si - me - on and An - na.   Arch - an - gels chant 'Ho -

chant 'Ho - san - na,   Ho - san - na, Ho - san - na!'

Arch - an - gels chant 'Ho - san - na!'

san - na!'   Arch - an - gels chant 'Ho - san - na!'

52

GOOD CHRISTIANS ALL, REJOICE

Text: John Mason Neale (1818-1866)
Music: Melody from Klug's *Geistliche Lieder*, 1535 (but earlier)
arranged by Robert Lucas Pearsall (1795-1856) and Christopher Tambling (*b.* 1964)

1. Good Christ-ians all, re - joice with heart and soul and voice!
2. Good Christ-ians all, re - joice with heart and soul and voice!
3. Good Christ-ians all, re - joice with heart and soul and voice!

Lis - ten now to what we say: Je - sus Christ is born to-day;
Hear the news of end - less bliss, Je - sus Christ was born for this;
Now you need not fear the grave, Je - sus Christ was born to save;

ox and ass be - fore him bow, and he is in the man - ger now.
he has o - pened hea-ven's door, and we are blessed for e - ver-more.
come at his most gra - cious call to find sal - va - tion, one and all:

Christ is born to day, Christ is born to day!
Christ was born for this, Christ was born for this.
Christ was born to save, Christ was born to save!

53
LO! HE COMES WITH CLOUDS DESCENDING

Text: Charles Wesley (1707-1788) and John Cennick (1718-1755)
Music: English Melody (18 c.) Last verse descant by Richard Lloyd (b.1933)

1. Lo! he comes with clouds de - scen - ding,
2. Ev - 'ry eye shall now be - hold him
3. Those dear to - kens of his pas - sion

once for fa - voured sin - ners slain; thou - sand
robed in dread - ful ma - jes - ty; those who
still his dazz - ling bo - dy bears, cause of

thou - sand saints at - tend - ing swell the
set at nought and sold him, pierced and
end - less ex - ul - ta - tion to his

tri - umph of his train: Al - le -
nailed him to the tree, deep - ly
ran - somed wor - ship - pers: with what

lu - ia! Al - le - lu - ia! Al - le -
wail - ing, deep - ly wail - ing, deep - ly
rap - ture, with what rap - ture, with what

lu - ia! God ap - pears on earth to reign.
wail - ing, shall the true Mes - si - ah see.
rap - ture gaze we on those glo - rious scars!

see over for verse 4

king - dom for thine own: Al - le -

king - dom for thine own: Al - le -

lu - ia! Al - le - lu - ia! Al - le -

lu - ia! Al - le - lu - ia! Al - le -

lu - ia! Al - le - lu - ia! Come, Lord, come!

lu - ia! Al - le - lu - ia! Come, Lord, come!

54
HUSH, MY DEAR, LIE STILL

Text: Isaac Watts (1674-1748)
Music: Malcolm Archer (b.1952)

1. Hush! my dear, lie still and slum - ber;
2. Sleep - ing babe; thy food and rai - ment,
3. Soft and ea - sy is thy cra - dle;
4. See the love - ly babe ad - dress - ing:

ho - ly an - gels guard thy bed! Heav'n - ly bless - ings
house and home, thy friends pro - vide; all with - out thy
coarse and hard thy Sa - viour lay when his birth - place
love - ly in - fant, how he smiled! when he wept, the

with - out num - ber gent - ly fall - ing on thy head.
care and pay - ment all thy wants are well sup - plied.
was a sta - ble and his soft - est bed was hay.
mo - ther's bless - ing soothed and hushed the ho - ly child.

Refrain

Lul - la - by, lul - la - by, hush, my ba - by, lul - la - by,

55

O COME, EMMANUEL

Text: Translated from the Latin by John Mason Neale (1818-1866)
Music: Adapted from a French Missal by Thomas Helmore (1811-1890)
arranged by Dom Gregory Murray (1905-1992)

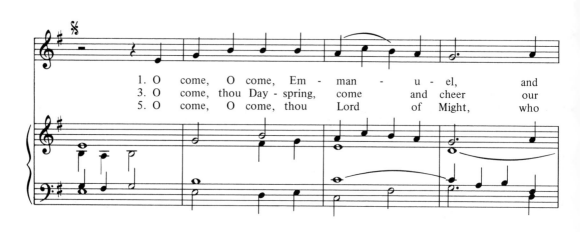

1. O come, O come, Em - man - u - el, and
3. O come, thou Day - spring, come and cheer our
5. O come, O come, thou Lord of Might, who

ran - som cap - tive Is - ra - el that
spi - rits by thine ad - vent here; dis -
to thy tribes on Si - nai's height in

mourns in lone - ly ex - ile here un - til the Son of
perse the gloom - y clouds of night, and death's dark sha - dows
an - cient times didst give the Law in cloud and ma - jes -

Refrain

God ap - pear.
put to flight. Re - joice, re - joice, O
ty and awe.

Is - ra - el, thy God shall come, Em - man - u -

Verses 2 and 4 | *Last time*

Verses 2 and 4

el. el.

Arranger's note: The music of the Refrain here follows the version as originally written by Thomas
Helmore. To change it on the plea that it is plainsong (which it manifestly is not)
is to destroy the rhythmical balance with the first two musical lines of the verse.

2. O come, thou Rod of Jes - se,
4. O come, thou Key of Da - vid,

free   thine   own from Sa - tan's   ty -   ran - ny;   from
come   and   o - pen wide our heav'n - ly   home;   make

depths of hell thy peo - ple save,   and   give them vic - t'ry
safe the way that   leads   on high,   and   close the path to

o'er   the grave.
mi - se - ry.

Refrain

Re - joice,   re - joice,   O

Is - ra - el, thy God shall come, Em - man - u -

D.S.

el.

Optional Refrain adapted by Alan Ridout

Re - joice, re - joice, O Is - ra - el, thy

Last time

God shall come, Em - man - u - el. - el.

56

I SING OF A MAIDEN

Text: Traditional (15 *c.*)
Music: Alan Ridout (*b.* 1934)

I sing of a maid-en that is make-less, King of all

kings to her son she ches. He
He came all so still

came all so still when his mo-ther was as dew in

A-pril that fall-eth on the grass. He
He came all so still

makeless = matchless; ches = chose

came all so still to his mo - ther's bower, as dew in

A - pril that fall -eth on the flower. He came all so still when his

mo -ther lay, as dew in A - pril that fall -eth on the

spray. Mo- ther and maid -en was ne - ver none but she:

well may such a la - dy God's mo - ther be.

57

For the Southwest Concert Choir

THE ROYAL CHILD

Text: John Keble (1711-1786)
Music: Adrian Vernon Fish (*b.*1956)

man - ger laid, the hope and glo - ry of all lands

man - ger laid, the hope and glo - ry of all

man - ger laid, the hope and glo - ry

is come, is come, come to the world's aid: no

lands is come, is come, come to the world's aid: no

of all lands is come, is come, come to the world's aid: no

peace - ful home up - on his cra - dle smiled; guests rude - ly went and

peace - ful home up - on his cra - dle smiled; guests rude - ly

peace - ful home up - on his cra - dle smiled; guests

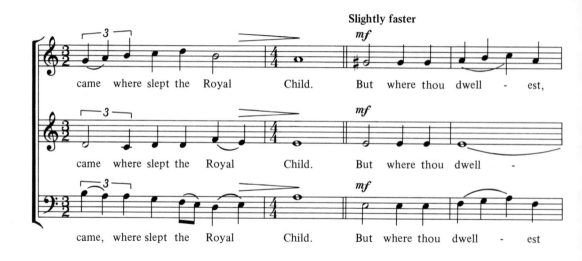

came where slept the Royal Child. But where thou dwell - est,
came where slept the Royal Child. But where thou dwell -
came, where slept the Royal Child. But where thou dwell - est

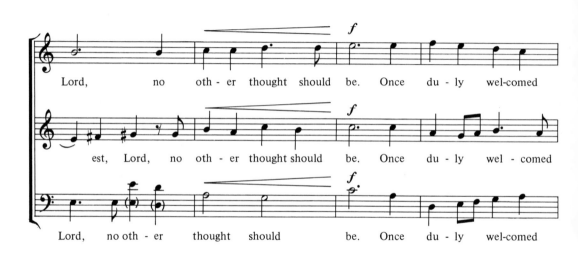

Lord, no oth - er thought should be. Once du - ly wel-comed
est, Lord, no oth - er thought should be. Once du - ly wel - comed
Lord, no oth - er thought should be. Once du - ly wel-comed

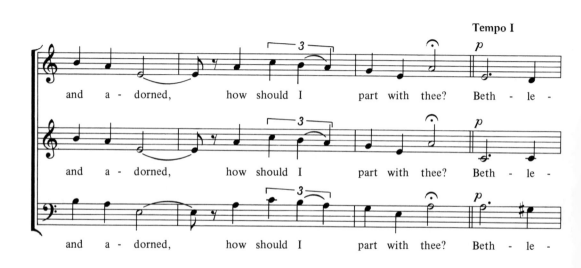

and a - dorned, how should I part with thee? Beth - le -
and a - dorned, how should I part with thee? Beth - le -
and a - dorned, how should I part with thee? Beth - le -

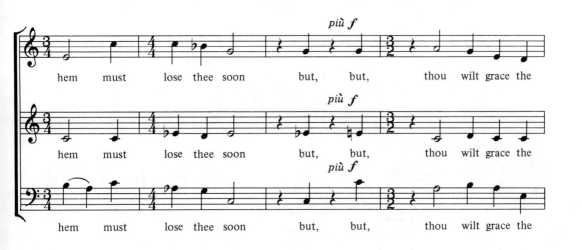

hem must lose thee soon but, but, thou wilt grace the

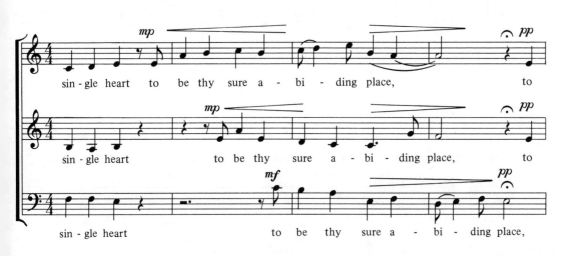

sin - gle heart to be thy sure a - bi - ding place, to

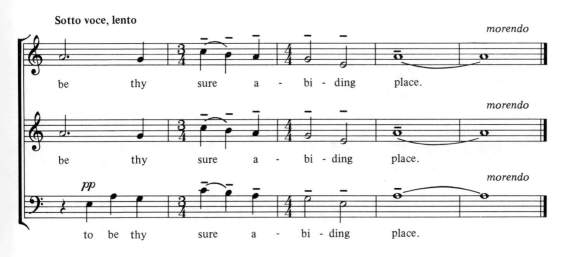

be thy sure a - bi - ding place.

225

58
O LITTLE TOWN OF BETHLEHEM

Text: Philips Brooks (1835-1893)
Music: Walford Davies (1869-1941) arranged by Harrison Oxley (*b.*1933)

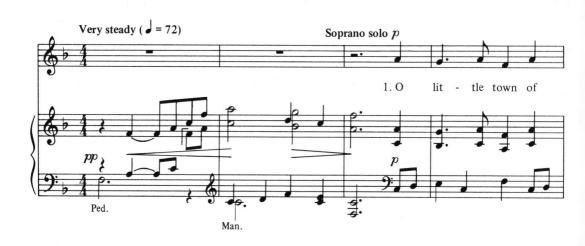

1. O lit - tle town of

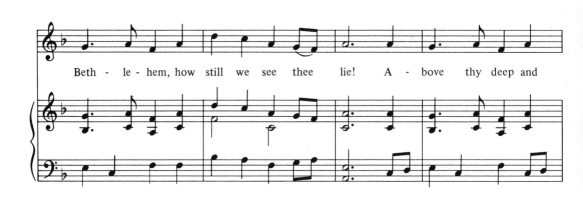

Beth - le - hem, how still we see thee lie! A - bove thy deep and

dream-less sleep the si - lent stars go by; yet in thy dark streets

shi - neth the e - ver - last - ing light; the hopes and fears of

all the years are met in thee to - night.

mf 2. O morn - ing stars, to - ge - ther pro -
pp 3. How si - lent - ly, how si - lent - ly the

mf 2. O morn - ing stars, to - ge - ther pro -
pp 3. How si - lent - ly, how si - lent - ly the

mf 2. O morn - ing stars, to - ge - ther pro -
pp 3. How si - lent - ly, how si - lent - ly the

mf
(*pp* 2nd time)

Man.

claim the ho-ly birth, and prai-ses sing to God the King, and
won-drous gift is giv'n! So God im-parts to hu-man hearts the

claim the ho-ly birth, and prai-ses sing to God the King, and
won-drous gift is giv'n! So God im-parts to hu-man hearts the

claim the ho-ly birth, and prai-ses sing to God the King, and
won-drous gift is giv'n! So God im-parts to hu-man hearts the

(cresc. 2nd time)

peace to men on earth. For Christ is born of Ma - ry; and
bless-ings of his heav'n. No ear may hear his com - ing; but

(cresc. 2nd time)

peace to men on earth. For Christ is born of Ma - ry; and
bless-ings of his heav'n. No ear may hear his com - ing; but

(cresc. 2nd time)

peace to men on earth. For Christ is born of Ma - ry; and
bless-ings of his heav'n. No ear may hear his com - ing; but

(cresc. 2nd time)

ga - thered all a - bove, while mor - tals sleep, the an - gels keep their
in this world of sin, where meek souls will re - ceive him, still the

watch of won - d'ring love.
dear Christ en - ters in.

Ped.
Man.

229

230

an - gels the great glad ti -dings tell: O come, O

an - gels the great glad ti -dings tell: O

come to us, a -bide with us, our Lord Em -

come to us, a -bide with us, our Lord Em -

man - u - el.

man - u - el.

Man.

231

59

O LITTLE TOWN OF BETHLEHEM

Text: Phillips Brooks (1835-1893)
Music: Traditional English Melody
collected and harmonised by Ralph Vaughan Williams (1872-1958)
Last verse descant by Thomas Armstrong (*b.*1898)

1. O lit - tle town of Beth - le - hem, how still we see thee
2. O morn - ing stars, to - ge - ther pro - claim the ho - ly
3. How si - lent - ly, how si - lent - ly, the won - drous gift is

lie! A - bove thy deep and dream - less sleep the si - lent stars go
birth, and prai - ses sing to God the King, and peace to men on
giv'n! So God im - parts to hu - man hearts the bless - ings of his

by. Yet in thy dark streets shin - eth the e - ver - last - ing
earth; for Christ is born of Ma - ry; and, ga - thered all a -
heav'n. No ear may hear his com - ing; but in this world of

light; the hopes and fears of all the years are met in thee to - night.
bove, while mor- tals sleep, the an - gels keep their watch of wond'ring love.
sin, where meek souls will re - ceive him, still the dear Christ en -ters in.

Descant

4. O ho - ly Child of Beth - le - hem, des - cend to us, we

All other voices

4. O ho - ly Child of Beth - le - hem, des - cend to us, we

pray; cast out our sin, and en - ter in, be

pray; cast out our sin, and en - ter in, be

born in us to - day. We hear the Christ - mas

born in us to - day. We hear the Christ - mas

an - gels the great glad tid - ings tell; O

an - gels the great glad tid - ings tell; O

come to us, a - bide with us, our Lord Em - man - u - el.

come to us, a - bide with us, our Lord Em - man - u - el.

60

THE LITTLE CRADLE ROCKS TONIGHT

Text and Music: American spiritual arranged by Michael Paget (*b.* 1936)

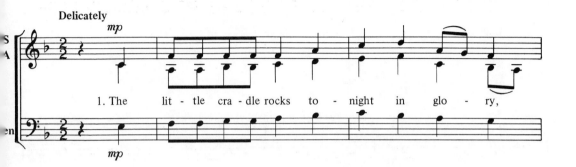

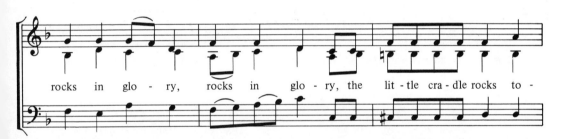

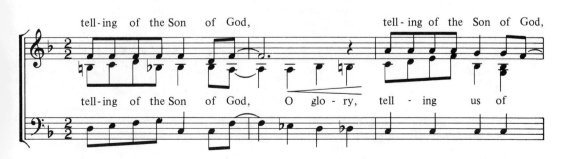

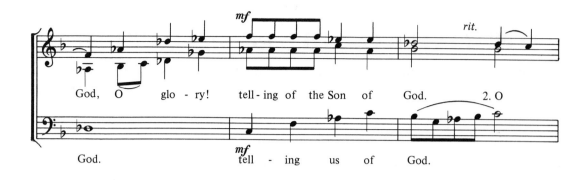

God, O glo - ry! tell - ing of the Son of God. 2. O

God. tell - ing us of God.

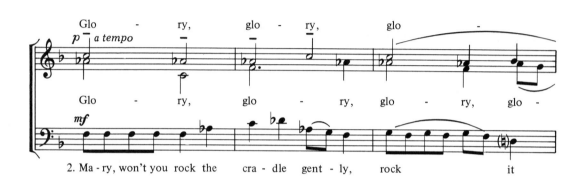

Glo - ry, glo - ry, glo -

Glo - ry, glo - ry, glo - ry, glo -

2. Ma - ry, won't you rock the cra - dle gent - ly, rock it

ry, glo - ry, glo - ry.

ry, glo - ry, glo - ry.

gent - ly, gent - ly. Ma - ry, won't you rock the cra - dle gent - ly,

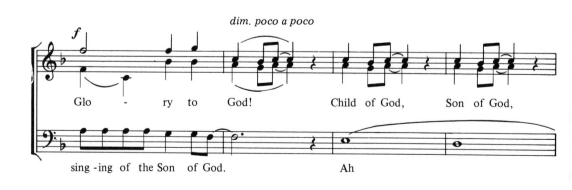

Glo - ry to God! Child of God, Son of God,

sing - ing of the Son of God. Ah

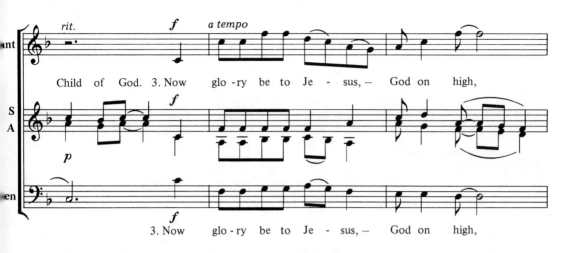

Child of God. 3. Now glo-ry be to Je - sus, — God on high,

3. Now glo-ry be to Je - sus, — God on high,

God on high, God on high, now glo - ry be to

God on high. God on high, now glo-ry be to Je - sus,

God on high. God on high, now glo - ry be to

God on high, bring-ing us to peace on earth. A - men.

God on high, bring-ing us to peace on earth. A - men.

61

MYN LIKING

Text: From the *Sloane* Manuscript (*c.*15 *c.*)
Music: Richard Runciman Terry (1865-1938)
arranged by Harrison Oxley (*b.*1933)

1. I saw a fair maid - en sit - ten and sing: she
lul - led a lit - tle child, a swee - te lord - ing.

240

Sopranos and Altos

mf

3. There was mick - le me - lo - dy at that child - es birth.

cresc. *molto rall.*

All that were in heav'n - ly bliss, they made mick - le mirth.

Refrain
mp a tempo

Solo

Lul - lay myn lik - ing, my dear son, my sweet - ing,

S
A
pp

Lul - la - lay, lul - la - lay,

pp
Lul - la - lay, lul - la - lay,

a tempo
pp

241

lul - lay my dear heart, mine own dear dar - ling.

own dear dar - ling.

lul - lay, my dear heart, mine own dear dar - ling.

lul - lay mine own dear dar - ling.

242

Fine

To Refrain ✛

Men
mf

4. An - gels bright   sang   their   song   to   that   child;   Bless -

cresc. molto rit.

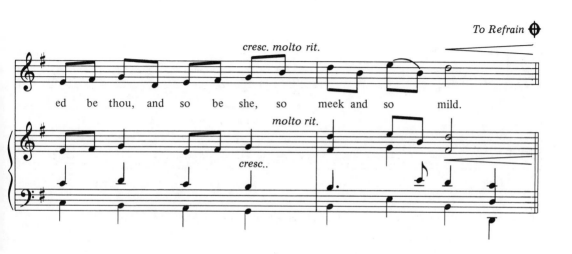

ed   be thou, and   so   be she,   so   meek and   so   mild.

molto rit.

cresc..

243

62

PAST THREE O'CLOCK

Text: George Ratcliffe Woodward (1848-1934)
Music: Traditional English Melody arranged by John Jordan (*b.* 1941)

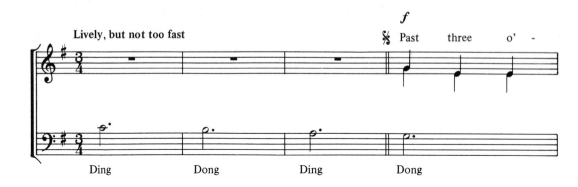

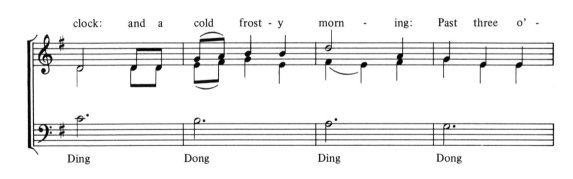

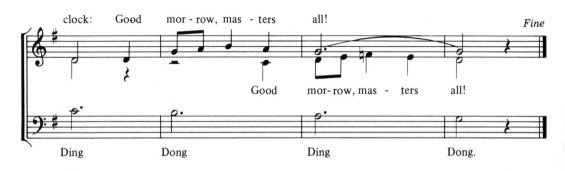

The verses may be varied by the altos and men singing 'Ah', or by using the organ.

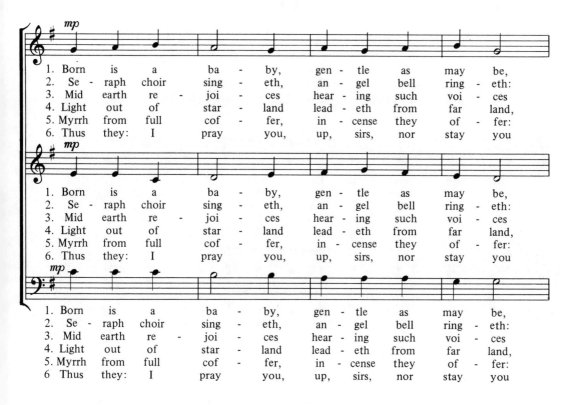

1. Born is a ba - by, gen - tle as may be,
2. Se - raph choir sing - eth, an - gel bell ring - eth:
3. Mid earth re - joi - ces hear - ing such voi - ces
4. Light out of star - land lead - eth from far land,
5. Myrrh from full cof - fer, in - cense they of - fer:
6. Thus they: I pray you, up, sirs, nor stay you

1. Born is a ba - by, gen - tle as may be,
2. Se - raph choir sing - eth, an - gel bell ring - eth:
3. Mid earth re - joi - ces hear - ing such voi - ces
4. Light out of star - land lead - eth from far land,
5. Myrrh from full cof - fer, in - cense they of - fer:
6. Thus they: I pray you, up, sirs, nor stay you

1. Born is a ba - by, gen - tle as may be,
2. Se - raph choir sing - eth, an - gel bell ring - eth:
3. Mid earth re - joi - ces hear - ing such voi - ces
4. Light out of star - land lead - eth from far land,
5. Myrrh from full cof - fer, in - cense they of - fer:
6 Thus they: I pray you, up, sirs, nor stay you

1. son of th'e - ter - nal Fa - ther su - per - nal.
2. hark how they rhyme it, time it, and chime it.
3. ne'er - to - fore so well ca - rol - ling 'Now - ell!'
4. prin - ces, to meet him, wor - ship and greet him.
5. nor is the gold - en nug - get with - hol - den.
6. till ye con - fess him, like - wise, and bless him.

1. son of th'e - ter - nal Fa - ther su - per - nal.
2. hark how they rhyme it, time it, and chime it.
3. ne'er - to - fore so well ca - rol - ling 'Now - ell!'
4. prin - ces, to meet him, wor - ship and greet him.
5. nor is the gold - en nug - get with - hol - den.
6. till ye con - fess him, like - wise, and bless him.

1. son of th'e - ter - nal Fa - ther su - per - nal. Ding
2. hark how they rhyme it, time it, and chime it. Ding
3. ne'er - to - fore so well ca - rol - ling 'Now - ell!' Ding
4. prin - ces, to meet him, wor - ship and greet him. Ding
5. nor is the gold - en nug - get with - hol - den. Ding
6. till ye con - fess him, like - wise, and bless him. Ding

63

ONCE IN ROYAL DAVID'S CITY

Text: Cecil Frances Alexander (1818-1895)
Music: Henry John Gauntlett (1805-1876)
Last verse descant by Richard Lloyd (*b.*1933)

1. Once in roy - al Da - vid's ci - ty stood a low - ly cat - tle shed, where a mo - ther laid her ba - by in a man - ger for his bed. Ma - ry
2. He came down to earth from hea - ven who is God and Lord of all, and his shel - ter was a sta - ble, and his cra - dle was a stall. With the
3. And through all his won - drous child - hood he would hon - our and o - bey, love, and watch the low - ly mai - den in whose gen - tle arms he lay; christ - ian
4. For he is our child - hood's pat - tern, day by day like us he grew; he was lit - tle, weak and help - less, tears and smiles like us he knew; and he
5. And our eyes at last shall see him through his own re - deem - ing love; for that child so dear and gen - tle is our Lord in heav'n a - bove; and he

was that mo-ther mild, Je-sus Christ her lit-tle child.
poor and mean and low-ly, lived on earth our Sa-viour ho-ly.
child-ren all must be mild, o-be-dient, good as he.
feel-eth for our sad-ness and he shar-eth in our glad-ness.
leads his child-ren on to the place where he is gone.

Descant

6. Not in that poor low-ly sta-ble, with the

All other voices

6. Not in that poor low-ly sta-ble, with the

ox-en stand-ing by, we shall see him, but in

ox-en stand-ing by, we shall see him, but in

hea - ven, set at God's right hand on high; where, like

hea - ven, set at God's right hand on high; where, like

stars his child - ren crown'd, all in white shall wait a - round.

stars his child - ren crown'd, all in white shall wait a - round.

64

WHEN JESUS CHRIST WAS YET A CHILD

Text: Plechtchéev translated by Geoffrey Dearmer (b.1893)
Music: Peter Ilich Tchaikovsky (1840-1893) arranged by Harrison Oxley (b.1933)

small and wild, where-in he cher-ished ro-ses fair,

and wove them in - to gar-lands there. 2. Now once, as

sum - mer-time drew nigh, there came a troop of

child - ren by, and see - ing ro - ses on the

tree, with shouts they plucked them mer - ri - ly.

3. 'Do you bind ro - ses in your hair?' they cried in

3. 'Do you bind ro - ses in your hair?' they cried in

3. 'Do you bind ro - ses in your hair?' they cried in

scorn to Je - sus there. The boy said hum - bly:

scorn to Je - sus there. The boy said hum - bly:

scorn to Je - sus there. The boy said hum - bly:

S
A
'Take, I pray, all but the na - ked thorns a -

Men

way.' 4. Then of the thorns they made a crown, and

Man.

252

with rough fin - gers pressed it down, till on his

fore - head fair and young red drops of blood like

ro - ses sprung, like ro - ses sprung.

65

THE VIRGIN MARY HAD A BABY BOY

Text and Music: Traditional West Indian Carol
arranged by Christopher Tambling (*b.*1964)

1. The Vir - gin Ma - ry had a ba - by boy, the

Vir - gin Ma - ry had a ba - by boy, the

Vir - gin Ma - ry had a ba - by boy, and they

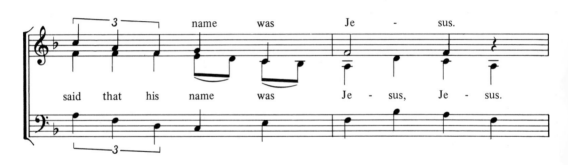

name was Je - sus.

said that his name was Je - sus, Je - sus.

He came from the glo - ry, glo - ry, he came from the glo - ri - ous king - dom. He came from the glo - ry, glo - ry, he came from the glo - ri - ous king - dom. 2. The

ah ah
an - gels sang when the ba - by was born, the an - gels sang when the
ah ah

the an - gels
ba - by was born, the an - gels sang when the ba - by was born, and pro -
the an - gels

66
SING OF A GIRL

Text: Damian Lundy (*b.* 1944)
Music: English Folk Melody arranged by Malcolm Archer (*b.* 1952)

With movement (♩. = 96)

S.A. 1. Sing of a
Men 2. Sing of a
S.A. 4. Sing of the
All 6. Sing of a

girl in the ri - pen - ing wheat, flow'rs in her
girl that the an - gels sur - round, dust in her
girl that a new man will meet, hand in his
girl who will ne - ver grow old, joy in her

hand, the sun in her hair. All the
hand, and straw in her hair. Kings and their
hand, the wind in her hair. Joy will
eyes and gold in her hair. Through the

world will run to her feet for the
crowns will fall to the ground be - fore the
rise as gold - en as wheat with the
a - ges men will be told of the

Last time to
Coda ❖

D.S. for verse 2

child that mo - ther will bear.
child that mo - ther will bear.
child that mo - ther will bear.
child that mo - ther will bear.

Descant

Ah

All other voices

3. Sing of a girl on a hill - side a - lone,
5. Sing of a girl in a cir - cle of love,

259

Ah

blood on her hand, and grey in her hair.
fire on her head, the light in her hair.

Ah   Ah

Sing of a bo - dy bro - ken and torn.   O,   the
Sing of the hearts the spi - rit will move   to love the

D.S. ⊕ CODA

Ah

child that mo - ther will bear!
child that mo - ther will bear!

rall.

L.H.

Ped.

67

AS JOSEPH WAS A-WALKING

Text: Traditional English Carol, adapted by Malcolm Archer (*b.* 1952)
Music: Richard Runciman Terry (1865-1938)
arranged by Christopher Tambling (*b.* 1964)

Refrain

As Jo - seph was a - walk - ing he heard an an - gel sing: 'This night is born to Ma - ry our heav'n - ly king!'

1. He
2. He
3. He

1. nei - ther shall be born in house nor in hall, nor in a place of pa - ra - dise, but in an ox - en stall. No - well, no - well.
2. nei - ther shall be co - vered in clo - thing rich and rare, but in the sim - ple lin - en which all the ba - bies wear. No - well, no - well.
3. nei - ther shall be rocked in sil - ver nor in gold, but in the wood - en man - ger which rocks up - on the mould. No - well, no - well.

68

AS WITH GLADNESS MEN OF OLD

Text: William Chatterton Dix (1837-1898)
Music: From a chorale by Conrad Kocher (1786-1872)
abridged by William Henry Monk (1823-1889)
Last verse descant by Malcolm Archer (b. 1952)

1. As with glad-ness men of old did the guid-ing star be-hold
2. As with joy-ful steps they sped to that low-ly man-ger bed,
3. As they of-fered gifts most rare at that man-ger rude and bare,
4. Ho-ly Je-su, ev-'ry day keep us in the nar-row way;

as with joy they hailed its light, lead-ing on-ward, beam-ing bright,
there to bend the knee be-fore him whom heav'n and earth a-dore,
so may we with ho-ly joy, pure, and free from sin's al-loy,
and, when earth-ly things are past, bring our ran-somed soul at last

so, most gra-cious God, may we e-ver-more be led to thee.
so may we with will-ing feet e-ver seek thy mer-cy-seat.
all our cost-liest trea-sures bring, Christ, to thee our heav'n-ly king.
where they need no star to guide, where no clouds thy glo-ry hide.

Descant

5. In the heav'n-ly coun - try bright need they no cre - a - ted light,

All other voices

5. In the heav'n - ly coun - try bright need they no cre - a - ted light,

Ped.

thou its joy, its crown, thou its sun which goes not down:

thou its light, its joy, its crown, thou its sun which goes not down:

there for e - ver may we sing al - le - lu - ias to our King.

there for e - ver may we sing al - le - lu - ias to our King.

69

THE SHEPHERD'S CRADLE SONG

Text: Translated from the German by A. Foxton Ferguson
Music: Karl Leuner (19 c.) arranged by Philip Moore (b.1943)

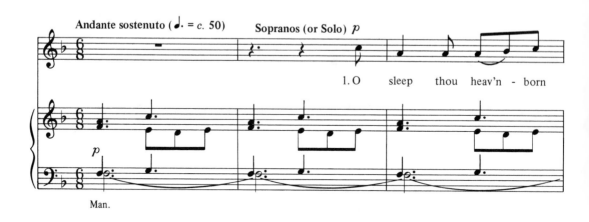

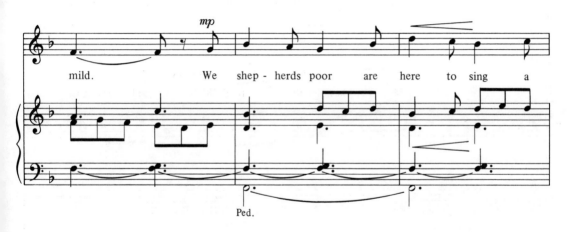

mild. We shep-herds poor are here to sing a

sim - ple lul - lay to our king. Lul - la - by,

lul - la - by, sleep, sleep soft - ly, lul - la - by.

2. See Ma - ry has with mo - ther's love a bed for thee out - spread, while Jo - seph stoops him from a - bove and watch - es at thy head, the lambs with - in the stall so nigh, that thou, may'st sleep, have hush'd their cry,

lul - la - by,   lul - la - by,   sleep, sleep soft - ly, lul - la -

by.   3. And when thou'rt big and art a man full

woe's   in store for thee;   for cru - el men thy

woe's   in store, in   store   for thee   for cru - el men thy

woe's   in store for   thee;   for cru -   el men thy

death will plan, and hang thee on a tree. So

Solo Sleep my ba - by, Lul -

S **A** sleep, my ba - by, whilst thou may, 'twill give thee rest a -

Men

70

ON JORDAN'S BANK

Text: Charles Coffin (1676-1749) translated by John Chandler (1808-1876)
Music: Adapted from a chorale in *Musicalisches Handbuch* (1690)
Last verse descant by Richard Lloyd (*b.*1933)

1. On Jordan's bank the Baptist's cry announces that the Lord is nigh; come then and hearken, for he brings glad tidings from the King of kings.

2. Then cleansed be ev'ry christian breast, and furnished for so great a guest! Yea, let us each our hearts prepare for Christ to come and enter there.

3. For thou art our salvation, Lord, our refuge and our great reward; without thy grace our souls must fade, and wither like a flow'r decayed.

4. Stretch forth thine hand to heal our sore, and make us rise, to fall no more; once more upon thy people shine, and fill the world with love divine.

Descant

5. All praise, e - ter - nal Son, to thee whose

All other voices

5. All praise, e - ter - nal Son, to thee whose

ad - vent sets thy peo - ple free, whom, with the Fa - ther,

ad - vent sets thy peo - ple free, whom, with the Fa - ther,

we a - dore, and Spi - rit blest, for e - ver - more.

we a - dore, and Spi - rit blest, for e - ver - more.

71

For Christ's Hospital

RAGTIME CAROL

Text: George Ratcliffe Woodward (1848-1934) (adapted)
Music: Christopher Tambling (b.1964)

1. Ding - dong, ding - dong, ding - dong, ding - dong, Up! Good Christ - en folk, and lis - ten,
2. Ding - dong, ding - dong, ding - dong, ding - dong, Tell the sto - ry how from glo - ry

how the mer-ry church bells ring, and from stee-ple
God came down at Christ-mas time, bring-ing glad-ness,

bid good peo-ple come and a-dore the new-born King:
chas-ing sad-ness, show-er-ing bless-ings far and wide.

3. Ding - dong, ding - dong, ding - dong,

ding - dong, ding - dong, ding - dong,

ding - dong, ding - dong, ding - dong,

ding - dong, ding - dong, ding - dong,

ding - dong, ding - dong, ding - dong,

Up! Good Christ - en folk and lis - ten, how the mer - ry church bells ring,

Up! Good Christ - en folk and lis - ten, how the mer - ry church bells ring,

ding - dong, ding - dong, ding - dong,

and from stee - ple bid good peo - ple

and from stee - ple bid good peo - ple ·

come and a - dore the new born King!

come and a - dore the new born King!

come and a - dore the new born King!

72

THE SNOW LAY ON THE GROUND

Text: Traditional English Carol
Music: Richard Runciman Terry (1865-1938)
arranged by Christopher Tambling (*b.* 1964)

1. The snow lay on the ground, the stars shone bright, when Christ our Lord was born on Christ - mas night.
2. 'Twas Ma - ry, daugh - ter pure of ho - ly Anne, that brought in - to the world the God made man.
3. She laid him in a stall at Beth - le - hem; the ass and ox - en shared the roof with them.
4. And Jo - seph, too, was by to tend the child, to guard him and pro - tect his mo - ther mild.
5. The an - gels ho - vered round and sang this song: 'Ve - ni - te a - do - re - mus Do - mi - num.'
6. And then that man - ger poor be - came a throne: for he whom Ma - ry bore was God the Son.
7. O come then let us join the heav'n - ly host, to praise the Fa - ther, Son, and Ho - ly Ghost.

73

For Bristol Cathedral Special Choir

THE LINDEN TREE CAROL

Text: Unknown, translated by George Ratcliffe Woodward (1848-1934)
Music: Malcolm Archer (*b.*1952)

1. There stood in heav'n a lin - den tree, but
3. 'Hail Ma - ry!' quoth the an - gel mild, 'Of
5. This ti - ding filled his friends with glee: 'Twas

tho' 'twas ho - ney - la - den, all
wo - man - kind the fair - est: the
passed from one to o - ther: ''Tis

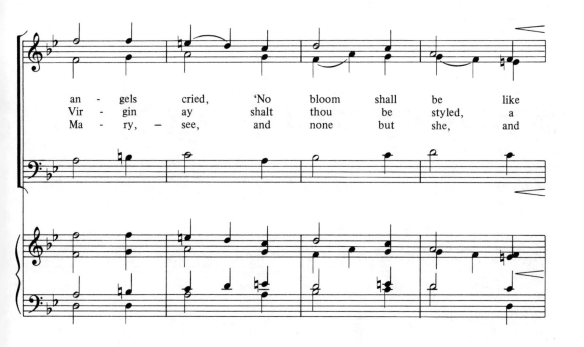

an - gels cried, 'No bloom shall be like
Vir - gin ay shalt thou be styled, a
Ma - ry, — see, and none but she, and

Fine

that of one fair maid - en.'
babe al - though thou bear - est.'
God will call her mo - ther.'

see over for verses 2 and 4

Solo Soprano

2. Sped Ga - bri - el on wing - ed feet, and
4. 'So be it!' God's hand - maid - en cried, 'Ac -

Man.

passed through bolt - ed por - tals, in
cord - ing to thy tell - ing,' where -

Na - za - reth, a maid to greet, blest
on the an - gel smart - ly hied up

o'er all o - ther mor - tals.
home - ward to his dwell - ing.

D.C.

280

74

A GREAT AND MIGHTY WONDER

Text: St. Germanus (634-732) translated by John Mason Neale (1818-1866)
Music: Old German Melody harmonised by Michael Praetorius (1571-1621)
arranged by Christopher Tambling (b. 1964)

1. A great and might-y won - der, a full and ho - ly
2. The Word be - comes in - car - nate and yet re - mains on
3. While thus they sing your mon - arch, those bright an - ge - lic
4. Since all he comes to ran - som, by all be he a -
5. And i - dol forms shall per - ish and er - ror shall de -

cure! The vir - gin bears the in - fant with
high! And che - ru - bim sing an - thems to
bands, re - joice, ye vales and moun - tains, ye
dored, the in - fant born in Beth - l'em, the
cay, and Christ shall wield his scep - tre, our

Refrain

vir - gin hon - our pure.
shep - herds from the sky.
o - ceans, clap your hands. Re - peat the hymn a - gain! To
Sa - viour and the Lord.
Lord and God for aye.

God on high be glo - ry, and peace on earth to men!'

75

THE FIRST NOWELL

Text: Traditional English Carol
Music: Traditional English Melody (*c.17c.*) arranged by Colin Mawby (*b.1936*)

1. The
2. They

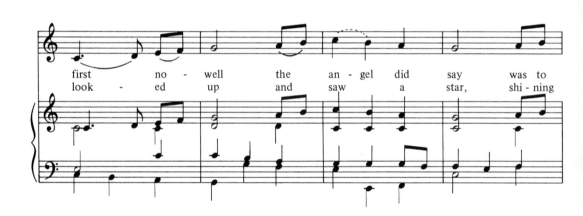

first no - well the an - gel did say was to
look - ed up and saw a star, shi - ning

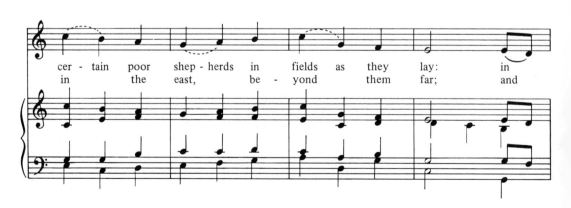

cer - tain poor shep - herds in fields as they lay: in
in the east, be - yond them far; and

fields where they lay, keep-ing their sheep, on a
to the earth it gave great light, on and

cold win - ter's night that was so deep.
so it con - tin - ued both day and night.

Refrain

No - well, no - well, no - well, no - well,

D.S.

born is the King of Is - ra - el!

283

3. And by the light of that same star three
wise men came from coun - try far, to
seek for a King was their in - tent and to
fol - low the star where - e - ver it went.

Refrain

No - well, no - well, no - well, no -

No - well, no - well, no - well, no -

well born is the King of Is - ra - el!

well born is the King of Is - ra - el!

Descant

4. This star drew nigh to the north - west, o'er

All other voices

4. This star drew nigh to the north - west, o'er

Beth - le - hem it took its rest, and
Beth - le - hem it took its rest, and

there it did both stop and stay right
there it did both stop and stay right

o - ver the place where Je - sus lay.
o - ver the place where Je - sus lay.

Refrain

no - well,   no - well,   no -

No - well,   no - well,   no - well,   no -

well,   born is the King of Is - ra - el!

well,   born is the King of Is - ra - el!

Unison

5. Then en - ter'd in those wise men three, full

rev - 'rent - ly up - on their knee, and of - fered

there in his pre - sence their gold and myrrh and

frank - in - cense.

Refrain

No - well, no - well, no - well, no -

well, born is the King of Is - ra - el!

Descant

6. Then let us all with one ac - cord sing prai - ses

Melody

6. Then let us all with one ac - cord sing prai - ses

to our heav'n - ly Lord, that hath made heav'n and

to our heav'n - ly Lord, that hath made heav'n and

earth of naught, and with his blood man - kind hath bought.

earth of naught, and with his blood man - kind hath bought.

76

BALULALOW

Text: John O'Hanlon (*b.*1941), based on a 15*c.* Scottish translation
of a Carol by Martin Luther (1483-1546)
Music: Malcolm Archer (*b.*1952)

1. My Je - sus, dear heart, my de - light, pre - pare thy cra - dle in my heart. Then
2. No, I will ne - ver cease my praise, my heart with-in me shall bend low: my

I will rock thee through the night and ne - ver from thy side de - part.
songs at once thy glo - ry raise, and lull thee with 'ba - lu - la - low!'

77

CHRISTIANS, AWAKE!

Text: John Byrom (1692-1763)
Music: John Wainwright (1723-1768) arranged by William Henry Monk (1823-1889)
Last verse descant by Richard Lloyd (b.1933)

1. Christ - ians, a - wake! Sa - lute the hap - py morn
2. Then to the watch - ful shep - herds it was told,
3. He spake; and straight - way the ce - les - tial choir
*4. To Beth - l'em straight th'en - light - ened shep - herds ran
*5. O may we keep and pon - der in our mind

where - on the Sa - viour of the world was born;
who heard th'an - ge - lic he - rald's voice, 'Be - hold,
in hymns of joy, un - known be - fore,' con - spire;
to see the won - der God had wrought for man,
God's won - drous love in sav - ing lost man - kind;

rise to a - dore the mys - te - ry of love
I bring you tid - ings of a Sa - viour's birth
the prai - ses of re - deem - ing love they sang,
and found, with Jo - seph and the bless - ed maid,
trace we the babe, who hath re - trieved our loss,

*This carol may be abridged, without affecting the sense of continuity, by omitting verses four and five.

which hosts of an - gels chant - ed from a - bove;
to you and all the na - tions on the earth;
and heaven's whole orb with al - le - lu - ias rang;
her Son, the Sa - viour, in a man - ger laid;
from his poor man - ger to his bit - ter cross;

with them the joy - ful tid - ings first be - gun, of
this day hath God ful - filled his pro - mised word, this
God's high - est glo - ry was their an - them still, peace
then to their flocks, still prai - sing God, re - turn, and
tread in his steps, as - sis - ted by his grace, till

God in - car - nate and the vir - gin's Son.
day is born a Sa - viour, Christ the Lord.'
up - on earth, and un - to men good - will.
their glad hearts with ho - ly rap - ture burn.
man's first heav'n - ly state a - gain takes place.

see over for verse 6

Descant

6. Then may we hope, th'an-ge-lic hosts a - mong,

All other voices

6. Then may we hope, th'an-ge-lic hosts a - mong,

to sing, re - deem'd, a glad tri - um-phal song:

to sing, re - deem'd, a glad tri - um - phal song:

He that was born up - on this joy - ful day, a - round us

He that was born up - on this joy - ful day

all,   a - round us all his glo - ry shall dis - play,

a - round us   all his glo - ry shall   dis -   play.

Saved   by his love, in - ces - sant we shall   sing

Saved   by his   love, in -   ces - sant we shall   sing   e -

e - ter - nal   praise,   al - migh -   ty   King.

ter -   nal   praise to heavn's al - migh -   ty   King.

78

BETHLEHEM CAROL

Text: Harrison Oxley (*b.*1933)
Music: Engelbert Humperdinck (1854-1921) arranged by Harrison Oxley

hushed and calm, far a - way all thought of harm.
all the earth; shep-herds saw, pro - claimed thy birth.

hushed and calm, far a - way all thought of harm.
all the earth; shep-herds saw, pro - claimed thy birth.

hushed and calm, far a - way all thought of harm.
all the earth; shep-herds saw, pro - claimed thy birth.

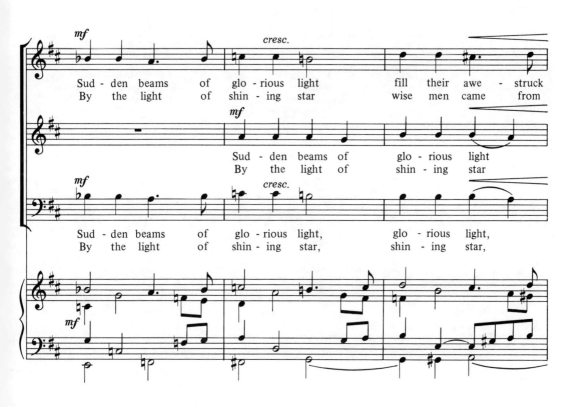

Sud - den beams of glo - rious light fill their awe - struck
By the light of shin - ing star wise men came from

Sud - den beams of glo - rious light
By the light of shin - ing star

Sud - den beams of glo - rious light,
By the light of shin - ing star,

297

hearts with fright! 'Fear not!' ring the voi - ces,
lands a - far, laid their gifts be - fore thee,

fill their awe - struck hearts with fright! 'Fear not!' ring the
wise men came from lands a - far, laid their gifts be -

fill their awe - struck hearts with fright!
wise men came from lands a - far,

pp subito

+ 16

Man.

poco cresc.
poco cresc.   *più cresc.*

'earth this day re - joi - ces! Go to find the
kneel - ing to a - dore thee. Bring me, Lord, their

poco cresc.   *più cresc.*

voi - ces, 'go to find the ho - ly
fore thee. Bring me, Lord, their joy to

p poco cresc.   *più cresc.*

'earth re - joi - ces! Go to find the
they a - dore thee. Bring me, Lord, to

poco cresc.

Ped.

298

ho - ly boy, born to fill the world with joy!'
joy to see, and give my lov - ing heart to thee.

boy, born to fill the world with joy!'
see, and give my heart to thee.

boy, born to fill the world with joy!'
see, and give my heart to thee.

79

SLEEP, HOLY CHILD

Text: Mark Woodruff (*b.* 1959)
Music: Traditional English Melody arranged by Alan Ridout (*b.* 1934)

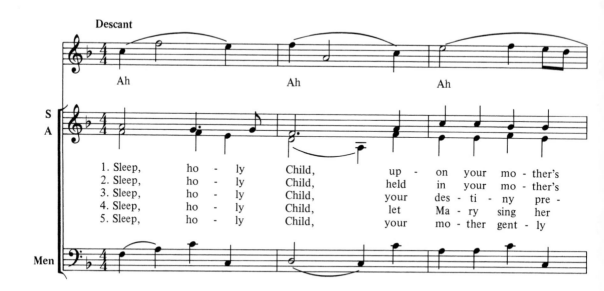

1. Sleep, ho - ly Child, up - on your mo - ther's
2. Sleep, ho - ly Child, held in your mo - ther's
3. Sleep, ho - ly Child, your des - ti - ny pre -
4. Sleep, ho - ly Child, let Ma - ry sing her
5. Sleep, ho - ly Child, your mo - ther gent - ly

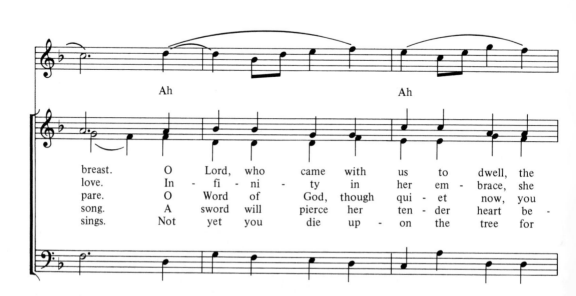

breast. O Lord, who came with us to dwell, the
love. In - fi - ni - ty in her em - brace, she
pare. O Word of God, though qui - et now, you
song. A sword will pierce her ten - der heart be -
sings. Not yet you die up - on the tree for

Ah   Ah   Ah   Ah

God of heav'n, Em - man - u - el, on earth in peace now rest.
guards with - in this si - lent place the Sa - viour from a - bove.
dream of teach - ing us to bow for love of God in prayer.
fore your death can grace im - part to rid us of our wrong.
us to live e - ter - nal - ly in heav'n, O King of kings.

80

LET ALL MORTAL FLESH KEEP SILENCE

Text: Liturgy of St. James translated by Gerard Moultrie (1829-1885)
Music: Traditional French Carol arranged by Dom Gregory Murray (1905-1992)

1. Let all mortal flesh keep silence and with fear and trembling stand; ponder nothing earthly minded, for with blessing in his hand Christ our God to earth de-
2. King of kings, yet born of Mary, as of old on earth he stood, Lord of lords, in human vesture, in the body and the blood: he will give to all the
3. Rank on rank the host of heaven spreads its vanguard on the way, as the light of light descendeth from the realms of endless day, that the pow'rs of hell may
4. At his feet the six-winged seraphs, cherubim with sleepless eye, veil their faces to the presence, as with ceaseless voice they cry, 'Alleluia, alle-

Verses 1, 2 and 3 | Last verse

scend - eth, our full hom-age to de - mand.
faith - ful his own self for heav'n-ly food.
van - ish as the dark-ness clears a - way.
lu - ia, al - le - lu - ia, Lord most high!'

Alternative Refrain, adapted by Alan Ridout

Descant

4. At his feet the che - ru - bim

S
A

4. At his feet the six - winged ser-aph; che-ru-bim with

Ped.

veil their fa-ces, as with cease-less voice they do cry, 'al-le-

sleep-less eye, veil their fa-ces to the pre-sence as with cease-less voice they cry,

lu - ia, al - le - lu - ia, Lord most high.'

'al - le - lu - ia, al - le - lu - ia, al - le - lu - ia, Lord most high.'

81

SUSSEX CAROL

Text: Traditional English Carol
Music: Traditional English Melody arranged by Malcolm Archer (*b.* 1952)

S.A. 1. On Christ - mas night all Christ - ians sing, to
2. why should men on earth be so sad, since

hear the news the an - gels bring, on Christ - mas night all
our re - deem - er made us glad, then why should men on

Christ - ians sing, to hear the news the an - gels bring;
earth be so sad since our re - deem - er made us glad,

f

news of great joy, news of great mirth,
when from our sin he set us free,

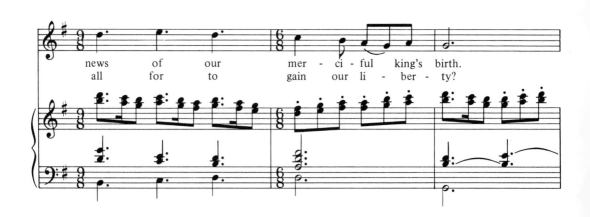

news of our mer - ci - ful king's birth.
all for to gain our li - ber - ty?

mp (v.3)

Men 2. Then
All 3. When sin de-parts be-

fore his grace, then life and health come in its place; when

sin de-parts; be - fore his grace, then life and health come in its place;

cresc.

an - gels and men with joy may sing, all for to

mf

we have light, which made the an - gels sing this night:

'Glo - ry to God and peace to men.

Now and for e - ver-more. A - men.'

82

A VIRGIN MOST PURE

Text: Traditional English Carol
Music: Traditional English Melody arranged by John Jordan (*b.* 1941)

1. A virgin most pure as the prophets do tell, hath brought forth a baby, as it hath be fell: to be our Redeemer from death, hell, and
2. In Bethlehem Jewry a city there was, where Joseph and Mary together did pass, and there to be taxed with many one
3. But when they had entered the city so fair, a number of people so mighty was there, that Joseph and Mary, whose substance was
4. Then they were constrained in a stable to lie, where horses and asses they used for to tie; their lodgings so simple they took it no
5. The King of all kings to this world being brought, small store of fine linen to wrap him was sought; and when she had swaddled her young son, so
6. Then God sent an angel from heaven so high to certain poor shepherds in fields where they lie, and bade them no longer in sorrow to
7. Then presently after the shepherds did spy a number of angels that stood in the sky; they joyfully talked and sweetly did

1. sin,   which   A - dam's   trans - gres - sion   had
2. mo,   for   Cae - sar   com - man - ded   the
3. small,   could   find   in   the   inn   there   no
4. scorn,   but a - gainst   the   next   morn - ing   our
5. sweet,   with - in   an   ox - man - ger   she
6. stay,   be - cause   that   our   Sa - viour   was
7. sing,   'To   God   be   all   glo - ry,   our

Refrain

1. wrap - ped us in.
2. same should be so.
3. lodg - ing at all.
4. Sa - viour was born. Aye, and there - fore be mer - ry: re -
5. laid him to sleep.
6. born on this day.
7. hea - ven - ly King.'

joice and be you mer - ry; set sor - row a - side; Christ

Je - sus our Sa - viour was born at this tide.

The verses may be varied by the altos and men singing 'Ah', or by using the organ.

83

OF THE FATHER'S LOVE BEGOTTEN

Text: Aurelius C. Prudentius (c. 348-413)
translated by John Mason Neale (1818-1866)
Music: Melody from *Piae Cantiones* (1582)
Last verse descant by Richard Lloyd (b.1933)

1. Of the Fa-ther's love be-got - ten ere the worlds be-gan to be, he is Al-pha and O-me - ga, he the source, the
2. At his word they were cre-a - ted; he com-mand-ed, it was done; heav'n and earth and depth of o - cean in their three-fold
3. O that birth for e-ver bless - ed when the Vir-gin, full of grace, by the Ho-ly Ghost con-ceiv - ing, bare the Sa-viour
4. O ye heights of heav'n, a-dore him, an-gel hosts, his prai - ses sing; pow'rs, do-mi-nions, bow be - fore him and ex-tol our
5. This is he whom seers and sa - ges sang of old with one ac-cord; whom the writ-ings of the pro - phets pro-mised in their

end - ing he, of the things that are, that have
or - der one; all that grows be - neath the shin -
of our race, and the babe, the world's re - deem -
God and King; let no tongue on earth be si -
faith - ful word; now he shines, the long ex - pec -

been, and the fu - ture years shall
- ing of the light of moon and
- er, first re - vealed his sa - cred
- lent, ev - 'ry voice in con - cert
- ted, let cre - a - tion praise its

see, e - ver - more and e - ver - more.
sun, e - ver - more and e - ver - more.
face, e - ver - more and e - ver - more.
ring, e - ver - more and e - ver - more.
Lord, e - ver - more and e - ver - more.

see over for verse 6

Descant

6. Christ, to thee, with God the Fa - ther, and, O

All other voices

6. Christ, to thee, with God the Fa - ther, and, O

Ho - ly Ghost, to thee hymn and chant and

Ho - ly Ghost, to thee hymn and chant and

high thanks - giv - ing and un - wear - ied

high thanks - giv - ing and un - wear - ied

prai - ses be, hon - our, glo - ry

prai - ses be, hon - our, glo - ry and do - min -

and do - min - ion, and e - ter - nal vic - to -

- ion, and e - ter - nal vic - to -

ry, e - ver - more and e - ver, e - ver - more.

ry, e - ver - more and e - ver - more.

84

For John Scott and the Choristers of St. Paul's Cathedral, London

VIRGIN-BORN, WE BOW BEFORE THEE

Text: Reginald Heber (1783-1826)
Music: Stanley Vann (*b.*1910)

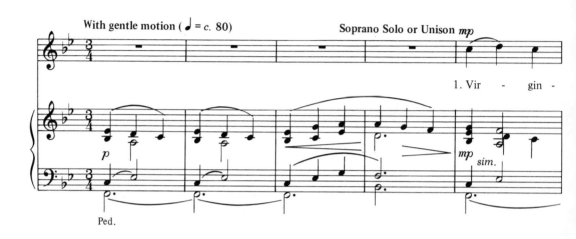

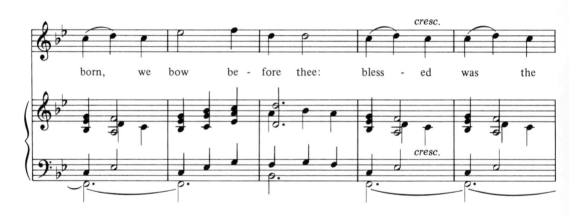

mild, bless - ed was she in her child.

Bless - ed was the breast that fed thee, bless - ed

was the hand that led thee; bless - ed was the

pa - rent's eye that watched thy slum - b'ring in - fan - cy.

2. Bless - ed she by all cre - a - tion, who brought forth the world's sal - va - tion, and bless- ed they, for e - ver blest, who love thee most and

serve thee best. Virgin born, we bow be - fore thee:

bless - ed was the womb that bore thee; Ma - ry, Mo - ther

meek and mild, bless - ed was she in her child.

85

SEE AMID THE WINTER'S SNOW

Text: Edward Caswall (1814-1878)
Music: John Goss (1800-1880) Descant by Alan Ridout (*b.* 1934)

1. See a-mid the win - ter's snow, born for us on earth be-low, see, the ten-der Lamb ap-pears, pro-mised from e-ter-nal years.
2. Lo, with-in a man-ger lies he who built the star-ry skies; he who, throned in heights sub-lime, sits a-mid the che-ru-bim.
3. Say, ye ho-ly shep-herds, say, what your joy-ful news to-day? Where-fore have ye left your sheep on the lone-ly moun-tain steep?
4. 'As we watched at dead of night, lo, we saw a won-drous light; an-gels, sing-ing peace on earth, told us of the Sa-viour's birth.'
5. Sa-cred in-fant, all di-vine, what a ten-der love was thine, thus to come from high-est bliss, down to such a world as this!
6. Teach, O teach us, ho-ly child, by thy face so meek and mild, teach us to re-sem-ble thee, in thy sweet hu-mi-li-ty.

Refrain

Descant

Hail, thou e - ver - bless - ed morn, hail, re - demp-tion's hap-py dawn!

Hail, thou e - ver - bless - ed morn, hail, re - demp-tion's hap-py dawn!

sing through all Je - ru - sa - lem, Christ is born in Beth - le - hem.

sing through all Je - ru - sa - lem, Christ is born in Beth - le - hem.

86
LORD JESUS HATH A GARDEN

Text: Jeremy Ashton (*b.* 1932) and others, based on a Dutch Carol
Music: Dutch Melody (1633) arranged by Philip Moore (*b.* 1943)

hea-ven-ly lyres, and de-li-cate lutes, with bright trum-pets, danc-ing cym-bals and the ten-der

D.C. for verse 2

sooth-ing flutes, with bright trum-pets, danc-ing cym-bals and the ten-der sooth-ing flutes.

p 3. The love-ly da-mask rose is pa-tience,
mf 5. But fair-est sight of all with-in those

flow'r so fair; the rich and fruit-ful ma-ri-gold, o-
walks and ways is Je-sus Christ, the gar-den-er, whom

Refrain

be - dience rare. Where an - gel choirs tune
an - gels praise.

hea-ven-ly lyres, and de-li-cate lutes, with bright trum - pets,

danc-ing cym-bals and the ten-der sooth-ing flutes, with

D.C. for verse 3

bright trum - pets, danc-ing cym-bals and the ten-der sooth-ing flutes.

6. Lord

6. Lord

Je - sus, these vir - tues bright shall make me whole; I

Je - sus, all these vir - tues bright shall make me whole; I

pray you make a gar - den fair of my poor soul: Where

pray you make a gar - den fair of my poor soul: Where

Refrain

an - gel choirs tune heav'n - ly lyres with bright trum - pets,

an - gel choirs tune hea - ven - ly lyres and de - li - cate lutes, with bright trum - pets,

bright
danc - ing cym - bals and the ten - der sooth - ing flutes, with bright trum - pets,

danc - ing cym - bals and the ten - der sooth - ing flutes, with bright trum - pets,

trum - pets
danc - ing cym - bals and the ten - der sooth - ing flutes.

danc - ing cym - bals and the ten - der sooth - ing flutes.

87

O LITTLE ONE SWEET

Text: Samuel Scheidt (1587-1684) translated by Percy Dearmer (1867-1936)
Music: German Melody from Samuel Scheidt's *Tabulaturbuch* (1650)
harmonised by Johann Sebastian Bach (1685-1750)
arranged by Christopher Tambling (*b.* 1964)

1. O little one sweet, O little one mild, thy Father's pur-pose thou hast ful-filled; thou cam'st from heav'n to mor-tal ken, e-qual to be with us poor men, O little one sweet, O little one mild.

2. O little one sweet, O little one mild, with joy thou hast the whole world filled; thou cam-est here from heav'n's do-main to bring men com-fort in their pain, O little one sweet, O little one mild.

3. O little one sweet, O little one mild, in thee love's beau-ties are all dis-tilled; then light in us thy love's bright flame, that we may give thee back the same, O little one sweet, O little one mild.

4. O little one sweet, O little one mild, help us to do as thou hast willed; lo, all we have be-longs to thee! Ah, keep us in our fe-al-ty! O little one sweet, O little one mild.

88

THE SHEPHERDS' FAREWELL

Text: Paul England (d.1932)
Music: Hector Berlioz (1803-1869), adapted by Christopher Tambling (b.1964)

hum - ble crib, the sta - ble bare, babe, all mor - tal
hum - ble love and ho - ly fear, in the land that
hap - py fa - ther, mo - ther mild! Guard ye well your

hum - ble crib, the sta - ble bare, babe, all mor - tal
hum - ble love and ho - ly fear, in the land that
hap - py fa - ther, mo - ther mild! Guard ye well your

hum - ble crib, the sta - ble bare, babe, all mor - tal
hum - ble love and ho - ly fear, in the land that
hap - py fa - ther, mo - ther mild! Guard ye well your

babes ex - cel - ling, con - tent our earth - ly lot to share,
lies be - fore thee for - get not us who lin - ger here!
heav'n - ly trea - sure, the Prince of Peace, the ho - ly child!

babes ex - cel - ling, con - tent our earth-ly lot to share,
lies be - fore thee for - get not us who lin - ger here!
heav'n - ly trea - sure, the Prince of Peace, the ho - ly child!

babes ex - cel - ling, con - tent our earth - ly lot to share,
lies be - fore thee for - get not us who lin - ger here!
heav'n - ly trea - sure, the Prince of Peace, the ho - ly child!

lov - ing fa - ther, lov - ing mo - ther shel - ter thee with
May the shep - herd's low - ly call - ing e - ver to thy
God go with you, God pro - tect you, guide you safe - ly

lov - ing fa - ther, lov - ing mo - ther shel - ter thee with
May the shep - herd's low - ly call - ing e - ver to thy
God go with you, God pro - tect you, guide you safe - ly

lov - ing fa - ther, lov - ing mo - ther shel - ter thee with
May the shep - herd's low - ly call - ing e - ver to thy
God go with you, God pro - tect you, guide you safe - ly

ten - der care! Lov - ing fa - ther, lov - ing mo - ther,
heart be dear! May the shep - herd's low - ly call - ing
through the wild! God go with you, God pro -tect you,

ten - der care! Lov - ing fa - ther, lov - ing mo - ther,
heart be dear! May the shep - herd's low - ly call - ing
through the wild! God go with you, God pro - tect you,

ten - der care! Lov - ing fa - ther, lov - ing mo - ther,
heart be dear! May the shep - herd's low - ly call - ing
through the wild! God go with you, God pro - tect you,

330

shel - ter thee with ten - der care, shel - ter thee with
e - ver to thy heart be dear, e - ver to thy
guide you safe - ly through the wild, guide you safe - ly

shel - ter thee with ten - der care, shel - ter thee with
e - ver to thy heart be dear, e - ver to thy
guide you safe - ly through the wild, guide you safe - ly

shel - ter thee with ten - der care, shel - ter thee with
e - ver to thy heart be dear, e - ver to thy
guide you safe - ly through the wild, guide you safe - ly

Verses 1 and 2 | Last verse

ten - der care!
heart be dear! through the wild!

ten - der care!
heart be dear! through the wild!

ten - der care!
heart be dear! through the wild!

Verses 1 and 2   D.C. | Last verse

331

89

UP! GOOD CHRISTEN FOLK

Text: George Ratcliffe Woodward (1848-1934)
Music: Melody from *Piae Cantiones* (1582) arranged by John Jordan (*b.*1941)

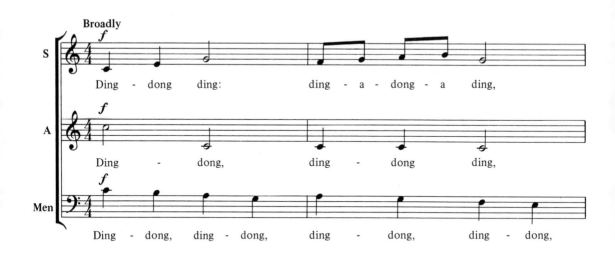

Ding - dong ding: ding - a - dong - a ding,

Ding - dong, ding - dong ding,

Ding - dong, ding - dong, ding - dong, ding - dong,

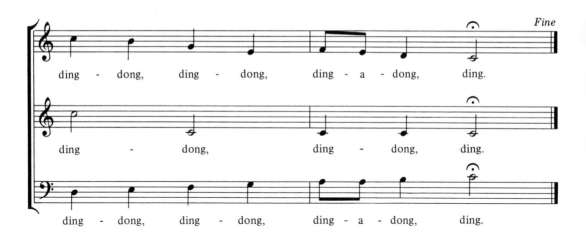

ding - dong, ding - dong, ding - a - dong, ding.

ding - dong, ding - dong, ding.

ding - dong, ding - dong, ding - a - dong, ding.

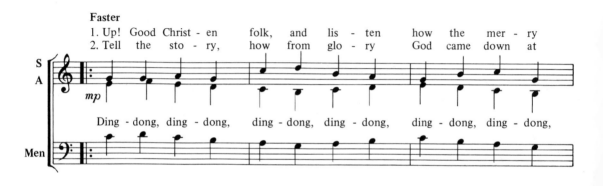

1. Up! Good Christ - en folk, and lis - ten how the mer - ry
2. Tell the sto - ry, how from glo - ry God came down at

Ding - dong, ding - dong, ding - dong, ding - dong, ding - dong, ding - dong,

church bells ring, and from stee - ple bid good peo - ple
Christ - mas - tide, bring - ing glad - ness, chas - ing sad - ness,

ding - dong, ding - dong, ding - dong ding, ding - dong, ding - dong, ding - dong, ding - dong,

come a - dore the new born King:
show - 'ring bless - ings far and wide.

ding - dong, ding - dong, ding - a - dong - a - ding - dong, ding - dong ding.
ding - dong ding - dong,

f

3. Born of mo - ther, blest o'er o - ther, ex Ma - ri - a

vir - gi - ne, *mf* in a sta - ble *p* ('tis no fa - ble,)

f D.C.

Christ - us na - tus ho - di - e.

333

90

SILENT NIGHT

Text: Joseph Mohr (1792-1848) translated by John Freeman Young (1820-1885)
Music: Franz Grüber (1787-1863) arranged by Colin Mawby (b.1936)

1. Si - lent night, ho - ly night. All is calm, all is bright,

round yon vir - gin mo - ther and child, ho - ly in - fant so

ten - der and mild: sleep in hea - ven - ly peace,

S
A

sleep in hea - ven - ly peace.

en

semplice

2. Si - lent night, ho - ly night. Shep - herds quake

at the sight, glo - ries stream from hea - ven a - far,

heav'n - ly hosts sing al - le - lu - ia: Christ the Sa - viour is

born, Christ the Sa - viour is born.

Descant

3. Si - lent night, ho - ly night. Son of God, love's pure light,

All other voices

3. Si - lent night, ho - ly night. Son of God, love's pure light,

ra - diant beams from thy ho - ly face, with the dawn of re - deem - ing grace:

ra - diant beams from thy ho - ly face, with the dawn of re - deem - ing grace:

Je - sus, Lord at thy birth. Je - sus, Lord, at thy birth.

Je - sus, Lord at thy birth. Je - sus, Lord, at thy birth.

91

PILGRIM CAROL

Text: Mark Woodruff (*b.* 1959)
Music: Song of the Shaker sect (*c.* 1840) arranged by Alan Ridout (*b.* 1934)

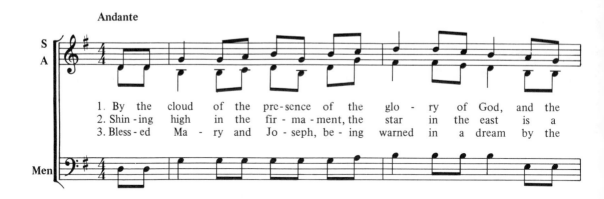

1. By the cloud of the pre-sence of the glo - ry of God, and the
2. Shin - ing high in the fir - ma - ment, the star in the east is a
3. Bless - ed Ma - ry and Jo - seph, be - ing warned in a dream by the

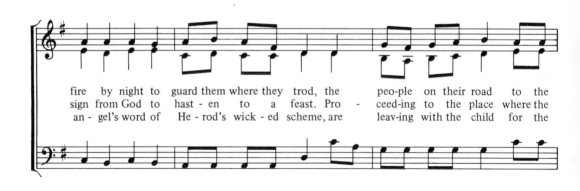

fire by night to guard them where they trod, the peo-ple on their road to the
sign from God to hast - en to a feast. Pro - ceed-ing to the place where the
an - gel's word of He - rod's wick - ed scheme, are leav-ing with the child for the

Pro - mised Land were trust - ing in God as he led them by hand.
in - fant lies, the wise men are led by the light in the skies.
ex - ile years, but Christ is their light and the hope in their fears.

Refrain

Descant

Ah   Ah

On - ward they fol - low to the end: they

Ah

faith - ful -ly heed their Fa - ther and friend. The jour - ney on may

Ah

lead far a - way, but they go with God as they trust and pray.

92

THE MOTHER OF JESUS

Text: Susan Sayers (*b.* 1946)
Music: Traditional French Melody arranged by Richard Lloyd (*b.* 1933)

1. The mo-ther of Je-sus gave birth to her Lord; the ba-by she

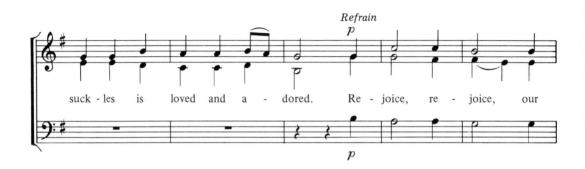

suck-les is loved and a-dored. Re-joice, re-joice, our

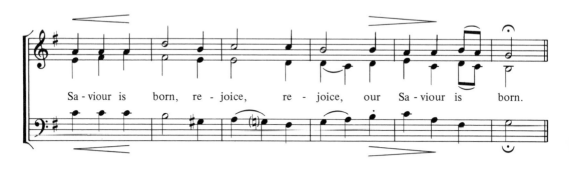

Sa-viour is born, re-joice, re-joice, our Sa-viour is born.

2. The Word of cre-a-tion, the Lord of all space, con-fined as a

Hum.

ba - by, looks up at her face. *Refrain* Re - joice, re - joice, our

Hum.

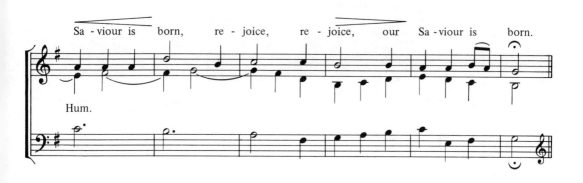

Sa - viour is born, re - joice, re - joice, our Sa - viour is born.

Hum.

S

3. The King of all peace lies a - sleep in her care; and kings kneel in

A

mp

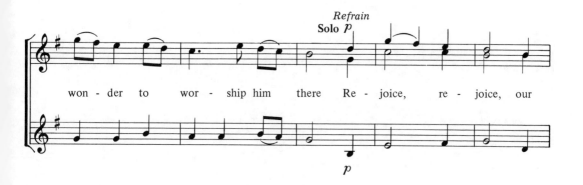

won - der to wor - ship him there *Refrain* Solo *p* Re - joice, re - joice, our

p

341

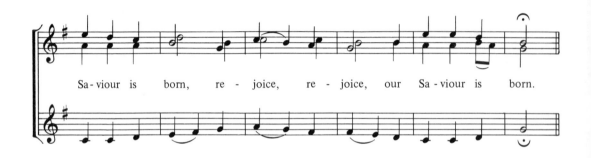

Sa - viour is born, re - joice, re - joice, our Sa - viour is born.

Altos *mf*

4. As Lord he will nou - rish the world with his bread; yet now by his

Men

mf

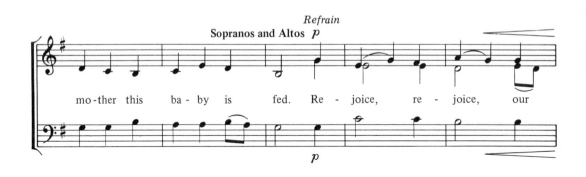

Refrain

Sopranos and Altos *p*

mo - ther this ba - by is fed. Re - joice, re - joice, our

p

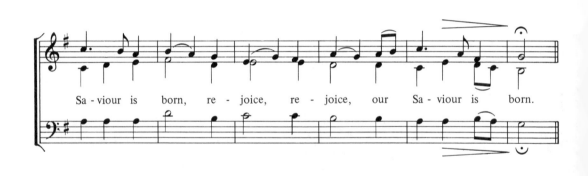

Sa - viour is born, re - joice, re - joice, our Sa - viour is born.

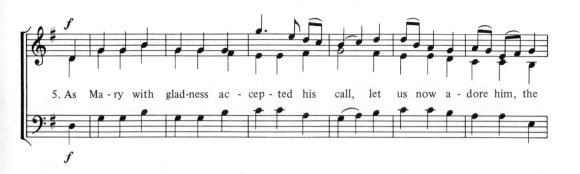

5. As Ma - ry with glad-ness ac - cep - ted his call, let us now a - dore him, the

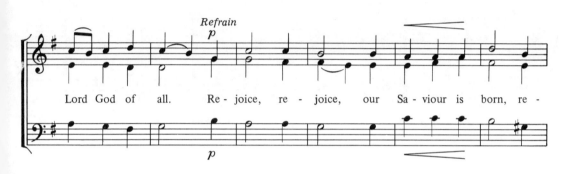

Refrain

Lord God of all. Re - joice, re - joice, our Sa - viour is born, re -

joice, re - joice, our Sa - viour is born. Re - joice, re - joice, our

Sa - viour is born, re - joice, re - joice, our Sa - viour is born.

93
FROM HEAVEN ABOVE

Text: Martin Luther (1483-1546)
Music: Graham Knott (b.1934)

SA 1. From heav'n a-bove to earth I come to bring good
Men 3. This is the Christ, God's Son most high, who hears your

Man.

news to ev-'ry-one! Glad ti - dings of great
sad and bit - ter cry; he will him-self your

joy I bring to all the world, and glad - ly sing.
Sa - viour be, and from all sin will set you free.

2. To you this night is born a
4. The bless - ing which the Fa - ther

(Organ)

child of Ma - ry, cho - sen vir - gin
planned the Son holds in his in - fant

mild; this new born child of
hand, that in his King - dom

low - ly birth shall be the joy of all the earth.
bright and fair, you may with us his glo - ry share.

All *f*

5. These are the signs which you will see to let you know that it is he: in man - ger bed, in swad - dling clothes, the child who all the earth up - holds.

più f

Ped.

rit.

94

SLEEP, BABY, SLEEP

Text: John Addington Symonds (1840-1893)
Music: Alan Ridout (*b.* 1934)

1. Sleep, ba - by, sleep! The mo - ther sings:
2. With swathes of scen - ted hay thy bed
3. At mid - night came the shep - herds, they
4. And three kings from the East a - far
5. They brought the gifts of gold and gems,
6. But thou who li - est slum - b'ring there,
7. Sleep, ba - by, sleep! The shep - herds sing:

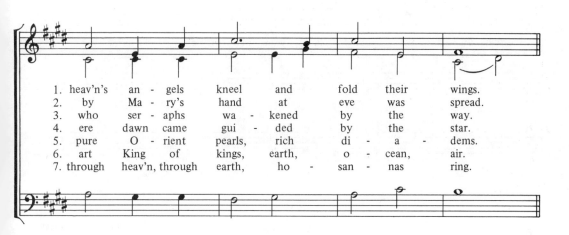

1. heav'n's an - gels kneel and fold their wings.
2. by Ma - ry's hand at eve was spread.
3. who ser - aphs wa - kened by the way.
4. ere dawn came gui - ded by the star.
5. pure O - rient pearls, rich di - a - dems.
6. art King of kings, earth, o - cean, air.
7. through heav'n, through earth, ho - san - nas ring.

Refrain

Sleep, ba - by, sleep, sleep, ba - by, sleep.

95

To the Choristers of Canterbury Cathedral, Christmas 1967

YE SHEPHERDS, LEAVE YOUR FLOCKS

Text: Source unknown
Music: Philip Moore (*b.* 1943)

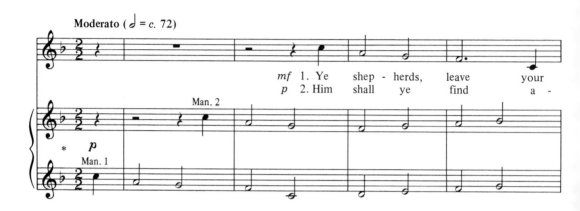

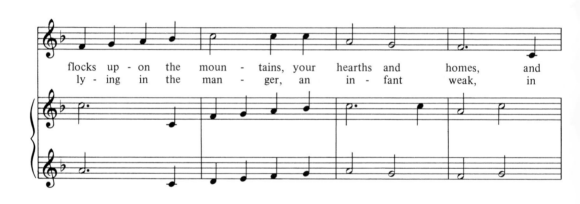

* This piece was originally arranged for two oboes and may be played thus.

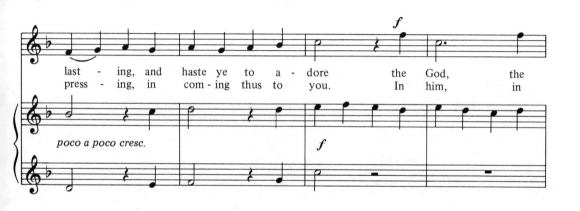

last - ing, and haste ye to a - dore the God, the
press - ing, in com - ing thus to you. In him, in

poco a poco cresc.

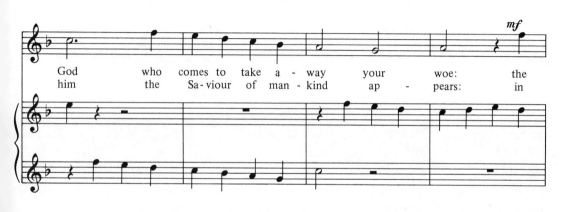

God who comes to take a - way your woe: the
him the Sa - viour of man - kind ap - pears: in

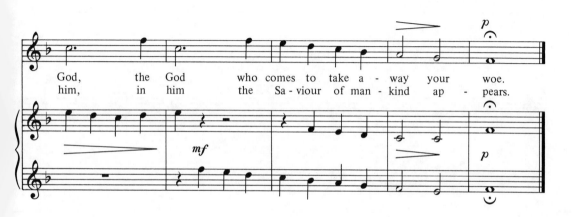

God, the God who comes to take a - way your woe.
him, in him the Sa - viour of man - kind ap - pears.

mf

96

SEE, TO US A CHILD IS BORN

Text: Timothy Dudley-Smith (*b.*1926) based on Isaiah 9: 6, 7
Music: Alan Ridout (*b.*1934)

1. See, to us a child is born; glo-ry breaks on Christ-mas morn!

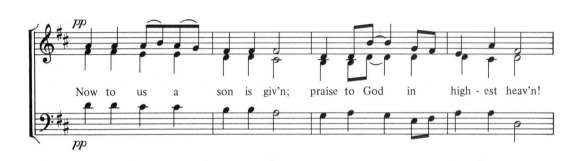

Now to us a son is giv'n; praise to God in high-est heav'n!

2. On his shoul-der rule shall rest; in him all the earth be blest!

Wise and won-der-ful his name; hea-ven's Lord in hu-man frame!

3. Might-ty God, who mer-cy brings; Lord of lords and King of kings!

Fa-ther of e-ter-nal days; ev-'ry crea-ture, sing his praise!

Descant

Ah!   Ah!

4. E-ver-last-ing Prince of peace; truth and right-eous-ness in-crease!

Ah!   Ah!   Ah!

He shall reign from shore to shore; Christ is King for e-ver-more!

97

WASSAIL SONG

Text: From Husk's *Songs of the Nativity* (1868)
Music: Traditional North of England Melody
arranged by Dom Gregory Murray (1905-1992)

1.
2. Our
3. We
4. Call

Here we came a was - sail - ing a - mong the leaves so green,
was - sail cup is made of the rose - ma - ry tree, and
are not dai - ly beg - gars that beg from door - to door, but
up the but - ler of this house, put on his gold - en ring;

Refrain

here we came a wan - der - ing, so fair to be seen;
so is your beer of the best bar - ley; Love and
we are neigh - bours' child - ren whom you have seen be - fore;
let him bring a glass of beer and bet - ter we shall sing;

joy come to you, and to you your was-sail too, and God

bless you, and send you a hap - py New Year, and God

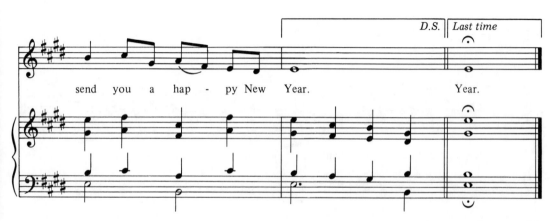

D.S. | Last time

send you a hap - py New Year. Year.

see over for verses 5-8
and alternative refrain

5.   We have got a lit - tle purse of stretch-ing lea - ther skin; we
6. Bring us out a ta - ble, and spread it with a cloth;
7. God bless the mas - ter of this house, like - wise the mis - tress too; and
8. Good mas - ter and good mis - tress, while you're sit - ting by the fire, pray

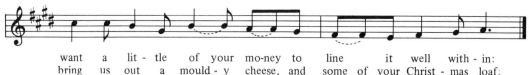

want a lit - tle of your mo-ney to line it well with - in:
bring us out a mould - y cheese, and some of your Christ - mas loaf:
all the lit - tle child - ren that round the ta - ble go:
think of us poor child - ren who are wand - 'ring in the mire:

Optional Refrain, adapted by Alan Ridout

S
A

Love and joy come to you, and to you your was-sail too, and God

Men

bless you, and send you a hap - py New Year, and God send you a hap - py New Year.

98
WHENCE IS THAT GOODLY FRAGRANCE?

Text: Translated from the French by Allen Beville Ramsay (1872-1955)
Music: Traditional French Carol arranged by John Sanders (b.1933)

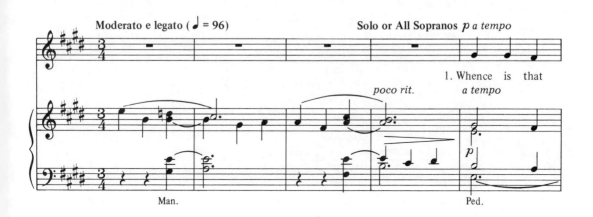

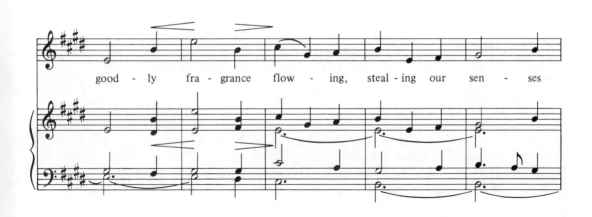

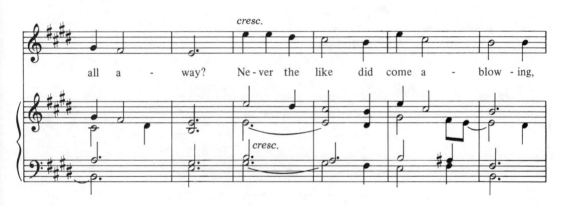

shep-herds, from flow-'ry fields in May. Whence is that good-ly

fra - grance flow - ing, steal-ing our sen - ses all a - way?

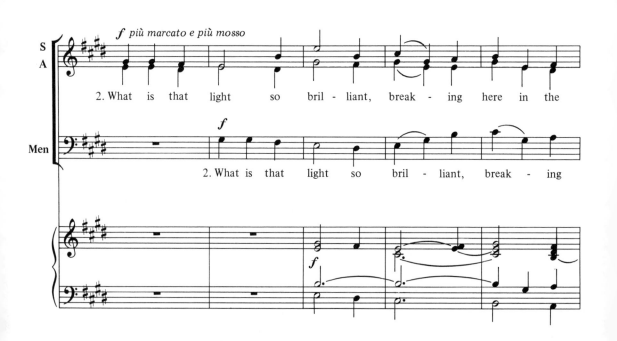

2. What is that light so bril - liant, break - ing here in the

2. What is that light so bril - liant, break - ing

night a - cross our eyes? Ne - ver so

here in the night a - cross our eyes. . Ne - ver so

Ne - ver so bright the day-star wak - ing start-ed to climb the

bright the day - star wak - ing start-ed to climb the morn - ing

poco rall.   *a tempo*

morn - ing skies.   *mf*

What is that light so bril - liant

mf

What is that light so

poco rall.   *a tempo*

break - ing here in the night a - cross our eyes.

bril - liant break - ing here in the night a - cross our eyes?

Tempo I e legato

3. Beth - le - hem! There in man - ger ly - ing, find your re -

deem - er, haste, a - way, run ye with ea - ger foot - steps

hie - ing! Wor - ship the Sa - viour born to - day!

Beth - le - hem! There in man - ger ly - ing, find your re -

deem - er, haste a - way!

99

LOVE CAME DOWN AT CHRISTMAS

Text: Christina Rossetti (1830-1894)
Music: Malcolm Archer (*b.* 1952)

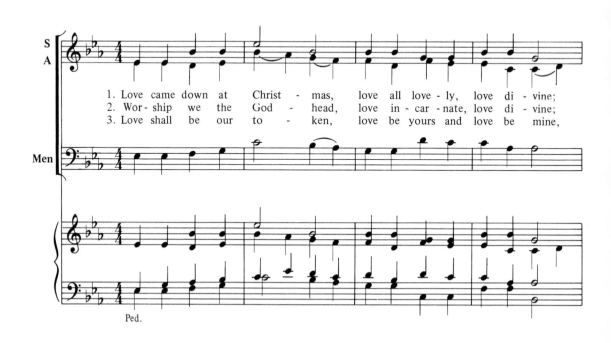

1. Love came down at Christ - mas, love all love - ly, love di - vine;
2. Wor - ship we the God - head, love in - car - nate, love di - vine;
3. Love shall be our to - ken, love be yours and love be mine,

love was born at Christ - mas, stars and an - gels gave the sign.
wor - ship we our Je - sus — but where - with for sa - cred sign?
love to God and all men, love for plea and gift and sign.

100

WE WISH YOU A MERRY CHRISTMAS

Text and Music: Traditional English West Country Carol
arranged by Colin Mawby (*b.*1936)

Presto. Non-delicato! Molto Inebriato! Moltissimo Raucouso!

Each chorister should conceal a small bottle of beer (or other drink) on stage. These should be opened at the end of this carol and a toast drunk to the audience.

kin; we wish you a mer-ry Christ-mas and a hap - py New Year!

kin; we wish you a mer-ry Christ-mas and a hap - py New Year!

Ped.

S
A

nasal gliss.

La, la, la, la, la, la, la, me - ow!

Men

half a bit-ter please. 2. Now

Man.

Gin and to - nic whis-ky and so - da now

bring us some fig-gy pud-ding, now bring us some fig - gy pud-ding, now

bring us some fig-gy pud-ding, and bring some *damn quick. Good

Refrain
Descant

All other voices

bring us some fig-gy pud-ding, and bring some out here. Good

Ped.　　　　　　　　　Man.

tid - ings we bring to you and your kin; we

tid - ings we bring to you and your kin; we

wish you a mer-ry Christ-mas and a hap - py New Year!

wish you a mer-ry Christ-mas and a hap - py New Year!

* ve-ry may be used as an alternative.

† At this point a flaming Christmas pudding should be brought to the choir.

Fig-gy pud-ding, tur-key and ham, woof, woof!

woof, woof! Where's our bit-ter please? 3. We

Hooch, hooch, no we don't, may-be we do,

Hooch, hooch, no we don't, may-be we do,

all like fig-gy pud-ding, we all like fig-gy

yes, yes, yes, we all like gin and to - nic, hick, so

yes, yes, yes, we all like gin and to - nic, hick, so

pud - ding, we all like fig - gy pud - ding, so

nasal gliss.

bring some, me - ow, wow. Hic, haec, hoc hunc, hanc, hoc,

nasal gliss.

bring some, me - ow, wow. Hic, haec, hoc hunc, hanc, hoc,

bring some out here. Good tid - ings we bring to

hu - jus, hu - jus. Where's our bit - ter, please? We wish you a mer - ry

Where's our bit - ter, please? We wish you a mer - ry

you and your kin, we wish you a mer - ry

S
A

Men

Christ - mas and a hap - py New Year. San - ta Claus

Christ - mas and a hap - py New Year. La, la, la,

Ped.

Man.

got some: Me - ow! hi! 4. We

la, what! Where's our as - te - risk bit - ter please? 4. We

won't go till we've got some, we won't go till we've got some, we

won't go till we've got some, so bring some out here. Good

Refrain

* Baroque choirs should double dot!